SLANGUAGE

Understanding American slang by coolest topic

I0435559

By:

Seyed Mahyar Shamsoddin

Acknowledgements

First and foremost my parents who have always given me the strength and wisdom to be sincere in my work, for setting high moral standards and supporting me through their hard work, and for their unselfish love and affection. This dissertation is dedicated to them.

Many thanks to fellow writer Slade J. Hunter for her time and encouragement

I would like to express my gratitude to the many people who saw me through this book; to all those who provided support, talked things over, read, wrote, offered comments, allowed me to quote their remarks and assisted in the editing, proofreading and design

Many thanks to http://all-free-download.com

Table of contents

Advice

bag your face
get lost
Example: bag your face . I don't wanna see you
again

beat it
go away
Example: How long you wanna stay here ! beat it!

break it up
stop it
Example: Break it up . I wanna got off

cheese it!
say someone to leave quickly
Example: Cheese it little boy!

chilax
chill , relax
Example: Just chilax and have a seat

chill out
to relax and take it easy
Example: Chill out man .

Chuck
To throw something.
Example: Just chuck the remote control over here,
will ya?

clam up!
be quiet
Example: Clam up and listen to teacher

come down
calm down
Example: come down dude . everything is gonna be all right

come off it
stop talking nonsense
Example: Oh , come off it ! that place is too expensive for us

cool it
relax , take it easy
Example: cool it dude

coop
To get rid of evidence quickly.
Example: Quick, your mom's coming. Coop your cigarette.

cut it out
stop it
Example: That's enough man , cut it out .

cut the comedy
be serious
Example: Cut the comedy and get to work

dig up
pay attention!
Example: Dig up man , this part is important

don't make fuss out of something
don't make something bigger matter
Example: Don't make fuss out of it . that was just like that

ease up on
To cease doing something.
Example: I told that stupid at the bar to ease up on the sauce.

easy does it
cool down
Example: You will win . easy does it

Flame On
to live up
Example: Hey Adam, flame on

get off it
stop saying nonsense
Example: Oh man , get off it , it was not my fault

get out of town
get out of the here
Example: Hey you , get out of town

get real
be pragmatic
Example: You can pass the exam . get real

get with it!
hurry up!
Example: Get with it! we wont get it there!

Give it a rest
stop talking nonsense
Example: Give it a rest , its all crap

give someone the lowdown
to inform someone
Example : I don't know what's happened , give me the lowdown

hang loose
relax . cool down
Example: Hang loose! that's not the one that you think

heads up !
look up because there is an object toward you
Example: Oh heads up!

hold your horses!
wait!
Example: Please get in line and hold your horses like everyone else

hustle!
hurry up
Example: hustle ! It's too late

keep it under one's hat
to keep a secret
Example: I think he is the boss . keep it under your hat

keep one's shirt on
be patient
Example: keep your shirt on man!

knock it off
stop that
Example: Knock it off , would you?

lets take a spin
Let's go
Example: Let's take a spin

make it snappy
hurry up , shake a leg
Example: Make it snappy and send me your photo

punch it
Let's go fast
Example: Okay then , punch it

put a sock in it
to shut someone's mouth
Example: Oh put a sock in it . stupid!

take a chill pill
be relax
Example: Take chill pill and don't think about it

Animal

a mouse in his pocket
Phrase used to describe someone large, probably very strong, but intensely stupid.
Example: We've got a new guy at work who worries me; I swear I think he's got a mouse in his pocket.

A pig in your pocket
Used when a person doesn't want to assist another.
Example: What do you mean we? Is there a pig in your pocket?

A real snake
a contemptible person
Example: Do you notice that your new girlfriend is a real
snake

alley cat
the cats are in street
Example: We have lots of alley cat in our neighborhood

antsy
restless
Example: He 's always so antsy

ape fest
rowdy party.
Example: Erasmus's birthday party was an ape-fest.

ape shit over something or someone
to go crazy with excitement for something or someone
Example: He apes shit over his girlfriend

arnoubi
little rabbit
Example: I love you, arnoubi.

as snug as a bug in a rug
extremely comfortable
Example: Were you comfortable in your new bed last
night ? yeah , It was as snug as a bug in a rug

bald as an eagle
very bald
Example: my uncle is bald as an eagle

batty
crazy
Example: You are such a batty

bean pole with chicken legs
a very tall man with thin legs
Example: He 's bean pole with chicken legs in our class

beat a dead horse
do something worthless
Example: I think he 's beating a dead horse now , he can't get that job

bee in one's bonnet
in a bad mood
Example: What's wrong with you? you have bee in your bonnet

big fish
boss , leader
Example: I'll asked my big fish if I can take the afternoon off

blind as a bat
very blind
Example: Without my glasses , I'm blind as a bat

Boonanimal
Describes an unattractive animal
Example: That's an ugly boonanimal

buffalo
to trick
Example: He buffaloed me!

buffed
muscular
Example: Who is that buffed over there?

bug
have cold
Example: I can't come to your party . because I got a bug

bull-headed
stubborn , obstinate
Example: He 's sick , but he 's too bull headed to see a doctor

bull shit
nonsense
Example: Stop talking bullshit please

busy as a beaver
extremely busy
Example: She 's always busy as a beaver

busy as a bee
extremely busy
Example: He never seems to have time to talk . he is busy as a bee

camel up
To get ready.
Example: Camel up before you go on a long walk.

cashcow
making profit
Example: ‹his year our company didn't make any cashcow

cat
backbiter
Example: I don't like to talk with cats

cat call
to say wise cracker to girls
Example: you should hear the cat calls she gets
whenever she walks down the street

cat soup
ketchup
Example: do you have a cat soup in your restaurant?

cat's whisker
very special person
Example: she thinks she is the cat whisker

catdude
Very cool person
Example: Clint Eastwood is a catdude.

catty
mean person
Example: don't trust on Rose , she is such a catty
person

chez-monkey
Someone who is dirty.
Example: Chris, you are a chez-monkey

chicken
timid guy
Example: Don't be a chicken man

chicken feed
small amount of money
Example: he lives with chicken feed

chicken leg
slender and thin leg
Example: all of his sons are chicken leg

chicken o'clock in the morning
really early, waking up with the chickens
Example: Ed's nuts! He wants to go fishing at
chicken o'clock in the morning.

chicken out
to lose one's courage
Example: he chicken out at the last minute

chickenhead
A woman who seeks men for their money.
Example: Ever since my pockets became fat, all
these chickenheads come swooping in trying to claim
my money.

chimneyfish
One who drinks a lot
Example: My dorm is inhabited by a bunch of
chimneyfish . It smells disgusting.

cock and bull story
ridiculous and unbelivable story
Example: every time I go to her house , his mother
tells me cock and bull story

coldfish
in a bad mood
Example: Tom is a coldfish . you can't talk to him
anytime

cooler than a cat
cool guy
Example: josh is cooler than a cat . he gave me his
car

copy cat
shark
Example: whatever I do , he 's trying to do the same .
what a copy cat he is!

couch monkey
Someone who just sits around and doesn't do much,
yet manages to make your life miserable.
Example: The couch monkeys in here won't let me
take any more vacation days

counter monkey
a waiter or waitress
Example: Sam is a counter monkey .

cow juice
milk cow
Example: I don't like cow juice at all . it makes me
feel blah

crazor, king of the monkey people
Someone truly insane, and unpleasant to be around.
Example: Stay away from Caleb. He's Crazor, king
of the monkey people

curiosity killed the cat
being too nosy may lead a person into trouble
Example: curiosity killed the cat

dead duck
predicament
Example: If you wanna stay here , your dead luck

dirty rat
a contemptible person
Example: you 're dirty rat! . I didn't know you!

dog
a close, trusted friend
Example: Tony and Lester Joe are my dogs- I'd trust them with anything

dog breath
what you have in the morning after a night of drinking a ton of beer smokin a pack of ciggs and whatever else
Example: Don't talk to me. get rid of that dog breath

dog do
excrement of dog
Example: Oh watched out , you walked on the dog do

dog-eat-dog
a very busy situation , very crowded
Example: It's a dog eat dog world out there

dog-tired
exhausted
Example: I'm going to bed . I'm dog tired

dognose
god knows
Example: A. Where's Johnny? B. Dognose. Probably in the pub

dogs
feet
Example: just go and wash your dogs!

dolphin clicking
When two people of similar interests can talk in a language that is not common.
Example: I'm really glad you two met; you seem to be dolphin clicking.

donkey
a stupid or silly person
Example: you donkey! hands off me!

donkey's year
long time , long year
Example: hey what's up dude? it's for a donkey years we haven't met each other

drunk as a skunk
extremely drunk
Example: he dank 4 glass of wine . now he 's drunk as a skunk

ducks
ticket
Example: how much did you pay for ducks?

eager beaver
extremely eager
Example: calm down ! you 're such an eager beaver

eagle eyes
said of a guy who is alert
Example: Tom is so eagle eyes . he never forgets
anything to bring with himself

eat a horse and chase the ride
hungry
Example: I'm so hungry I could eat a horse and chase
the rider.

eat like a horse
eat in a bad way
Example: she eats like a horse

eat like a pig
to overeat
Example: stop it! you eat like a pig!

edrolthiledge
a big bee.
Example: Don't move. That edrolthiledge might sting
you.

every dog has his day
every body should trust on god
Example: Don't worry , every dog has his day

fat cat
rich guy
Example: my older uncle is a fat cat in our folks

fat cow
extremely fat
Example: your new girlfriend is fat cow

fine kettle of fish
predicament
Example: that's a fine kettle of fish . what should we do now?

fish
hot guy
Example: Look at the fish twirling his mustache over there, standing in the corner.

fishy
suspicious
Example: You look fishy , what's happened?

flat out like a lizard drinkin
To be very busy.
Example: I've got all these projects to do , I'm flat out like a lizard drinking.

fly
intelligence
Example: we don't have any fly in our class

fly boy
pilot
Example: my friend is a fly boy

fly gear
wearing the finest clothes
Example: are you gonn'a go somewhere? no , so why u are fly gear?

gentle as a lamb
extremely kind and tender
Example: my dog is a gentle as a lamb

get goose egg
to receive something from someone very cheap
Example: what did you get for your birthday? I just
got goose egg

get somebody goat
to annoy someone
Example: Don't get my goat anymore . I'm listening
to music

goose someone
to pinch someone
Example: I was in the bus suddenly someone goose
me behind me

grease monkey
a mechanic
Example: my friend is a grease monkey

have a bee in one's bonnet
to be in a bad mood
Example: My friend has a bee in one's bonnet

have a cow
get upset
Example: Don't have a cow!

have a memory like an elephant
have a good brain to memory all things
Example: my friend has a memory like a elephant .
whatever I say he remembers

have ants in the pants
to be restless
Example: Do u have ants in your pants or what?

have bats in the belfry
to be crazy
Example: she 's got bats in the belfry

hen-pecked
a man who lets himself dominated by his wife
Example: john is a real hen pecked

hep cat
a very intelligent looking guy
Example: she met with a hep cat in the subway

hoggish
greedy
Example: don't be so hoggish and share with your brother

hogwash
nonsense
Example: that's a bunch of hogwash your saying

holy cow!
oh my god!
Example: holy cow! I forget to bring my house keys

horse around
to do nothing important
Example: stop horsing around and do something profitable

hungry as a wolf
extremely hungry
Example: hey just find a place to eat . I'm hungry as a wolf

in a pig's eye!
never
Example: would you ever go out with her? in a pig's eye

in a while crocodile
see you soon
Example: in a while crocodile dude .

in dog house
have a problem with talking to someone
Example: are you in dog house with your mom?

in hog heaven
in joy
Example: let's be in hog heaven and enjoy this party

in two shakes of a lamb's tail
in very quickly moment , very quickly
Example: In two shakes of a limb's tail she ate whole cake!

kicked by a horse
to become addicted to heroin
Example: since he 's lost his job , he 's kicked by a horse

lard
fat pig
Example: we have lots of lard in our farm

lone wolf
hermit
Example: when I was a kid , I was lone wolf in our family

lucky dog
lucky person
Example: you won the lottery! you are lucky dog man!

make a monkey out of someone
to make someone punk
Example: whenever I hang out with my friends , we make a monkey out of people in the street

make a mountain out of a molehill
to make issue bigger than the real condition that it is
Example: Don't make a mountain out of molehill

make fish eyes at someone
to look at someone with lots of love
Example: she made fish eyes at my little brother

meek as a mouse
extremely gentle and harmless
Example: Don't afraid of him . he 's a meek as a mouse

mind one's own bee's wax
to mind one's own business
Example: mind your own business!

monkey
playful , wanton
Example: she 's a really money in our class

monkey around
to prance
Example: stop making monkey around and go to study your lessons

monkey business
monkeyshine , trick
Example: try to earn money without doing monkey business

monkey suit
a suit for men
Example: he didn't wear monkey suit in his wedding

mousy
shy person
Example: she 's sort of a mousy

mutt
a dog
Example: I was chased by mutt yesterday

my dogs are barking
have a pain in feet
Example: my feet are hurting

night owl
a person who likes to stay up until late at night
Example: you are a real night owl man!

on one's high horse
acting like snobbish person
Example: one of my classmate is on his high horse

pig out
overeat
Example: I'm hungry . let's go out and pig out pizza!

pigeon
one who is really simple and is swindled
Example: Mike is so pigeon

pigheaded
stubborn
Example: you 're always so stubborn

pinky
the little finger
Example: he always wears ring in pinky

poker
pig
Example: hey look at that pig over there

pour one's money down a rat hole
to invest one's money in a none profitable venture , to throw away one's money
Example: If you invest in his company , you 're pouring your money down a rat hole

pussy cat
instead of say honey
Example: hi pussy cat . I'm home

put a bug in someone's ear
to alert someone about a news
Example: put a bug in your ears and listen what I say

put on the dog
wearing the finest clothes to go somewhere
Example: he put on the dog and went to party

quack
clumsy guy
Example: Greg is such a quack guy . he never could do anything with his hands

quit cold turkey
to quit bad habit
Example: when you want to quit cold turkey?

rabbit ears
antenna
Example: I buy new rabbit ears . but still have a problem with getting a good picture on television .

rain cats and dogs
a very heavy rain
Example: hey look at the weather , seems raining cats and dogs

rat
a horrible, nasty person
Example: there are lots of rat in our neighborhood

rat around
to screw around , waste time , fart around
Example: stop ratting around and come to help me here

rat fink
a contemptible person
Example: you rat fink

rat race
daily work routine
Example: well , I think it's time to go back into the
rat race

road hog
a driver who dominates the road
Example: my daddy is a road hog in this city . you
know?

rug rat
a very small child , infant
Example: It's really hard to take care of rug rat

scaredy cat
to be a coward
Example: whenever I see a dog , I'm scaredy cat

see you later alligator
see you soon
Example: see you later alligator

sheepish
embarrassed
Example: every since I scolded her , she 's been
acting very sheepish with me

sick as a dog
very ill
Example: he was sick as a dog and couldn't come to
work

silly goose
truly insane person
Example: she afraid of silly goose around here

slippey as a snake
sly and astute
Example: I don't trust him . he 's slippery as a snake

sly as a fox
be dishonest
Example: one of his friends act like sly as a fox

slydog
dishonest person
Example: he was slydog and stole all the money by his acting

smell a rat
to be suspicious
Example: I'm beginning to smell a rat here

spring chicken
youthful
Example: he is a spring chicken

squirrelly
fishy person
Example: you can't trust her . she a squirrely person

stool pigeon
backbiter
Example: you told her what happened?! you 're a stool pigeon!
informant

straw that broke the camel's back
boiling point
Example: the straw that broke the camel's back of
water is 212f or 100C .

take the bull by the horns
to take risk
Example: you've got to just take the bull by the horns
and tell them what you did

talk turkey
to talk straightforward and frank
Example: Ok , let's talk turkey with them

the cat's got your tongue?
when somebody doesn't talk we say this slang idiom
Example: why don't you talk? the cat's got your
tongue?

the early bird catches the worm
whoever gets up early accomplishes more
Example: the early bird catches the worm

throw a monkey wrench into something
to stop the process of something or something
Example: we were about to begin construction on the
building but they threw a monkey wrench into the
project

to buy a pig in a poke
to buy sth without seeing it first
Example: I don't like to buy a pig in a poke

top dog
to be head of a company
Example: he's top dog in this company

turkey
stupid
Example: turn off that turkey program!

until the cows come home
for long time , donkey years
Example: until the cows come home I haven't seen you , what's cooking dude?

watch like a hawk
watch very closely
Example: watch like a hawk and tell me what your seeing

whale
fat person
Example: my uncle is a whale

whale of a sth
an extraordinary
Example: I watched a whale of a movie yesterday

whale on someone
to beat someone
Example: Did you see her whale on her son in the market

when donkeys fly!
never
Example: Don't you want date him ? when donkeys fly!

when pigs fly!
never
Example: will you marry him? when pigs fly!

white elephant
an insignifacant object that is in house and serves no real purpose other than dust
Example: you know , she always like to have white elephants in her room

wise owl
a very knowing and clever person
Example: I like my brother . he 's a wise owl

wolf down something
to eat food in a hurry
Example: Don't wolf down your pizza . It's not late yet

work out all the bugs
to remedy all the problems
Example: My new invention is almost ready . I just need a few more hours to work out all the bugs

worm
a contemptible person
Example: you like him? he is a worm!

worm out of a situation
not to help someone
Example: he promised me to give me a hand . but finally he wormed out of a situation

worm something out of someone
to coax someone in order to get something from them
Example: I wasn't planning on telling her what
happened last night . but she wormed it out of me

zebra
referee
Example: john is a zebra in this soccer match

Annoyance

aggrannoyed
The point at which you become aggressive.
Example: She kept on and kept on about my dress
until I became aggrannoyed.

aggro
bother (n)
Example: That dog has never been a aggro to anyone

bug
to bother
Example: That girl bug me all the time

dental
painful, annoying.
Example: Going to the hospital is dental.

dirty
When something or someone is getting on your
nerves or bothers you.
Example: I sat for a dirty hour waiting on the station

drive somebody up a wall
to bother someone
Example: The kids are driving me up a wall

eat
to anger
Example: What's eating you today

eat one's up
to irritate someone
Example: That really eats me up

fed up
cant stand something anymore
Example: I'm fed up with this car

fess with someone
to annoy someone
Example I know you're doing this only to annoy me

fillerneumic peckerloomer
Someone who annoys you inordinately.
Example: That guy is a fillerneumic peckerloomer
for not being here on time.

fleen
Little bugs you don't know the names of.
Example: Get these fleens off me!

gag someone with a spoon
to hate something
Example: She gags me with a spoon

get all bent out of shape
to become very angry
Example: My dad got all bent out of shape when I came home late

get in someone's hair
to annoy
Example: My little brother keeps getting in my hair

get off someone's back
to annoy someone
Example: Get off my back please!

get ones back up
to make one irritated and angry
Example: I don't like her . She always gets my back up

get someone's goat
to irritate someone
Example: You know that nothing gets my goat more than when someone is late

give someone the willies
make someone nervous
Example: You 're giving me the willies

hassle
to annoy or bother someone
Example: hey kids! Stop it . you're hassling me

hound
to pester someone
Example: He hounded me to say whole story

on the edge
irritable
Example: The baby has really been irritable today.

rag on somebody
to harass , to annoy
Example: You always rag on me , knock it off

rattle
to upset or unnerve, to make someone feel nervous
Example: She likes to rattle people

rub someone the wrong way
annoy somebody
Example: She told him and it rubs her the wrong way

talk someone ear off
to irritate someone by talking too much
Example: She talked my ear off for a whole hour

tee off
to make someone angry, to annoy
Example: he tees off his father for asking him to buy him a car

ticked off
to be angry
Example: You seem really ticked off . what's up ?

touchy
irritable ,
Example: I know I'm just being touchy

Bird

a bird in hand is worth two in the bush
to be happy with what you got
Example: a bird in hand is worth two in the bush

a little birdie told me
when we know something , but its sort of a secret
how
we know it
Example: how did you get we got married? a little
birdie told me

bird brain
stupid
Example: Sam is a real bird brain

bird legs
very thin legs
Example: hey man you have become bird legs . have
something to eat!

bird watcher
eyeball , have rowing eyes
Example: Jack is a bird watcher

chicken
afraid
Example: at first he was chicken to get in the water

chicken out
decide not to do something because you are scared
Example: he chicken out to tell his wife he talked to
a lady

37

crankybird
A person in a foul mood.
Example: Jeeze, why are you being such a crankybird?

don't pull all your eggs in one basket
don't destroy all you chance that you've got
Example: Don't pull all your eggs in one basket

early bird
a person who gets up early in the morning
Example: my daddy is a early bird

eat like a bird
eat like birds
Example: he eats like a bird

for the birds
undesirable , nonsense
Example: I hate math , I think is for the birds

get all ones ducks in a row
become organized
Example: she really needed get all her ducks in a row

jailbird
prisoner
Example: he is jailbird

kill two birds with one stone
accomplish two things at the same time
Example: Finally , he could kill two birds with one stone

Body

absobloodlylutely
100% . certainly
Example: we will do it . absobloodlylutely

backne
acne on one's back and shoulders.
Example: Ewww! Ben's backne was so gross!

body factory
graveyard
Example: the hood that he lives is near body factory

body shake
to punish someone
Example: I was given a body shake in school

brainy
to be very intelligence
Example: his new girlfriend is such a brainy girl

crakne
a topical outbreak of acne confined to the buttocks.
Example: I shan't be wearing a thong to the beach
this evening as I have an unsightly case of crackne.

deuce
To poke someone in the eye with two fingers.
Example: Sometimes I wear a special face mask so
that I can't be deuced.

duster
ass , bottom
Example: move your duster and give it to me

elbow grease
hard work
Example: the stain will come off . it just takes some
elbow grease

elbow ones way
to make ones way through a crowd by pushing with
ones elbow
Example: I had to elbow my way through the crowd

fight tooth and nail
to fight violently
Example: I fought tooth and nail to stop the country
from condemning the library

flap one's gums
to talk nonsense
Example: stop flapping your gums!

Flobby
The state of lazy or very tired muscles which makes
moving difficult or impossible.
Example: After hiking up a long hill my daughter fell
to the ground claiming she was all flobby.

get nailed
to get in big trouble
Example: by transferring drugs into Armenia , he got
nailed .

get something off someone chest
to expose ones burdening feelings to someone
Example: I need to talk to you and get this off my chest

give someone elbow room
to give someone space
Example: I can hardly move . give me some elbow room

give someone the cold shoulder
not to speak to someone
Example: he is giving her friend the cold shoulder

give the shirt off one's back
to give all one can
Example: he'll give the shirt off his back for his friends

have one's teeth chatter
to shiver
Example: I'm so cold . my teeth are chattering

hold one's tongue
to stop talking
Example: hold your tongue please!

jump down one's throat
to attack someone verbally
Example: I gave her suggestion and she jumped down my throat

knuckle down
to get serious and stop playing
Example: we've got to knuckle down and clean this house

knuckle under
to surrender
Example: he finally knuckled under because the pressure was simply too much

mind your P's and Q's
be careful when talking
Example: mind your P's and Q's .

nail somebody on the wall
to put somebody under pressure
Example: the economical issues nailed him on the wall .

neck and neck
be even in a competition
Example: the two runners are neck and neck

nerve
audacity
Example: you have some nerve!

nerves on edge
to be overwrought
Example: I think I need a drink . my nerves are on edge

nervy
to have audacity
Example: she 's really nervy

on one's toe
alert
Example: there could be trouble , so be on your toes

ones right arm
ones valuable partner
Example: he is my right arm

over my dead body
Example: over my dead body!

pain in the neck
to be annoying
Example: your new friend is a pain in the neck . have you ever noticed?
to be annoying

palm off something on someone
to rid oneself of something undesirable by giving it to someone
Example: my brother palmed off his old bicycle on me

pick someone's brain
to question someone carefully in order to further ones own knowledge
Example: since you are an expert , would you mind if I pick your brain for an hour?

rack one's brain
to strain to remember something or find a solution to a problem
Example: I racked my brains for an hour but couldn't remember her name!

redneck
bigot , prejudiced
Example: he 's a real redneck

rest on one's shoulder
to depend on someone
Example: the job rests on your shoulder now

roll off one's back
not to affect someone
Example: she insulted me , but I just let it roll off my
back .

rub elbow with someone
to socialize with someone
Example: when I went to holly wood , I rubbed
elbows with all the movie stars

rubberneck
tourist
Example: If you like to meet rubberneck , you should
travel to Isfahan .

rusty-dusty
ass , duster
Example: do you know the meaning of rusty-dusty?

scatterbrain
one who is eccentric and flighty
Example: he is such a scatterbrain

set one's teeth on the edge
to make one shudder
Example: you dogs sit my teeth on the edge

shoot from the hip
to act or respond impulsively
Example: he never thinks before he speaks

speak a tongue
to speak a language
Example: how many tongue does she speak?

speak straight from the shoulder
to speak directly and straightforward
Example: I spoke straight from the shoulder and told him I didn't like the way he treated me

spineless
cowardly
Example: he was really angry at his boss but was afraid to tell him . sometimes he 's so spineless

strong arm someone
to force someone to do something
Example: he was strong armed into doing it

the cat's got your tongue?
 to be speechless or unable to talk
Example: why don 't you speak? the cat's got your tongue?

thumb a ride
to hitchhike
Example: since we ran out of gas , we were forced to thumb a ride into the city

thumbs up
approval
Example: he gave me a thumbs up on the project

tip toe around someone
to be cautious around someone
Example: she 's so unpredictable that you have to tip toe around her

to get down to the bar bone essential
to discuss the most important issues
Example lets get down to the bare bone essential

toe the line
to behave properly
Example: If he doesn't toe the line , fire him !

toe to toe
to fight
Example: they are going toe to toe

tongue in cheek
sarcastically
Example she said it tongue in cheek

tongue tied
to be speechless
Example: whenever I talk in front of an audience , I get tongue tied

tough as nail
very strong
Example several constructions will be tough as nail

turn one's back
to reject
Example he turned his back on me when i needed him

turn the other cheek
to accept without argument or resistance
Example: his mother turned the other cheek when he
took the cookie

twist ones arm
to force someone to do something
Example no ones twisting your arm to do it !

under one's thumb
under one's control
Example: he will do anything I ask . I have him
under my thumb

up in arms
angry
Example: you can't talk to him . he's up in arms .

walk arm in arm
to walk while holding each others arm
Example they always walk arm in arm down the
beach

wring someone's neck
to strangle someone
Example: if I catch him , I'm gonna wring his neck!

zits
pimple
Example: have you ever looked at mirror and see
your face? It has got so many zit .

Bone

bone up
to study or practice
Example: I need to bone up on my English

boney
so thin that ones bones show , very thin
Example: my girlfriend is boney

corpus-bones
This sucks. shit
Example: Corpus-bones! I can't believe we have to
do this. ah ,

crazy bone
arm
Example :I hit my crazy bone

have bone to pick with someone
to have a subject of disagreement , a conflict
Example: I have a bone to pick with you

lazy bone
an extremely lazy person
Example: wake up , lazy bone!

make no bones about something
absolutely , unquestionably , straightforward
Example: he made no bones about telling her to
leave

nothing but skin and bones
to be extremely thin
Example: he is nothing but skin and bones

Car

blowout
a ruptured tire
Example: Oh , I think I just got another blowout

brain bucket
A motorcycle helmet.
Example: You could have been hurt a lot worse in that accident if you hadn't been wearing a brain bucket

broadside
to hit the side of another car with the front of one's own car
Example: the driver next to me fell sleep and broadsided me!

brodey
to spin the car 180 degrees .
Example: since the road was so slippery , when I applied the brake hard , I did a brodey

bumper-to-bumper
said of heavy traffic
Example: the traffic was bumper-to-bumper all the way home

burn rubber
to accelerate so quickly
Example: he always likes to burn rubber with his new car

cabbie
a taxi driver, a cab driver
Example: her dad is a cabbie

dash
abbreviation of dashboard
Example: what do you have in your dash?

deuce coupe
car that seats only two people
Example: my friend has got a nice deuce coupe

eat one's dust
to be left behind by a fast moving car
Example: your gonna eat my dust!

fangio
A person driving dangerously
Example: Check out Fangio ,he's all over the road

fender bender
an insignificant traffic accident which causes little damage
Example: Don't worry , I'm okay , that was just a fender bender accident

flame-out
The engine on a vehicle stops abruptly, usually in the middle of traffic, or at a busy intersection
Example: My truck flamed-out downtown during rush hour this afternoon!

flipping a risky
to make an illegal U-turn in a high-traffic, highly visible city street
Example: Everybody hold on! I'm flipping a risky!

floor it
to push the accelerator all the way to the floor
Example: we cant get them man , you gotta floor it!

hop up
to improve the performance of the engine
Example: Due to not hop up the car , he lost the race

jalopy
old car , and old fashioned
Example: I just told to my father to sell this damn jalopy

jam on the brakes
to apply the brake in one quick motion .
Example: for avoiding to accident , he had to jam on the brakes

jump-start
to start one's car battery off someone else's battery
Example: my battery died but luckily we were able to start the car by jump-starting

leave in the dust
to pass someone quickly in a car
Example: we sure left them in the dust

lemon
unreliable car!
Example: you really bought a lemon

light it up
to start the engine
Example: we gotta get there as soon as possible .
Let's light it up

limo
limousine
Example: wow , check out that limo!

loaded
said of a car which is sold with many extras
Example: look at that loaded!

peel out
to accelerate quickly
Example: when they saw us coming , they peeled
out

pileup
an accident involving a number of cars
Example: lets avoid that street . I heard there was
just a pileup there

pop the clutch
to release the clutch quickly causing the car to lurch
forward
Example: I don't like to pop the clutch anytime

pull the pedal to the metal
to push the accelerator all the way to the metal floor
of the car
Example: in 5 minutes , I gotta be there , just pull
the pedal to the metal !

punch it
to accelerate quickly
Example: as soon as the light turns green , punch it!

put it in high gear
to move into high speed
Example: you gotta put it in high gear , otherwise
we are going to be late

rattletrap
old car
Example: what rattletrap you have man !

rev up
in order to make warm the car's engine
Example: you have to rev up the car before starting
to go

tail
(see bumper to bumper)
Example: we drove until get to Boston just in tail

wheels
a car
Example: Do you have a wheels?

Clothes

have ants in one's pants
to be squirmy and restless
Example: you always have ants in your pants!

beat the socks off someone
to win
Example: I won! I beat the socks off the others!

belt someone
to hit someone with the fist
Example: I will belt him if he wont refund my money

blue collar worker
one who does manual work
Example: my cousin is a blue collar worker

boot someone
to eject someone
Example: he booted me out of his room

boot up
to start up a computer
Example: I have to boot up computer in order to show you my project

chezt
To dress yourself.
Example: I'll be right back, I gotta go get chezted.

chotels
Tight shorts or pants that are like a cheap hotel
Example: Did you see the chotels on Chris? Give it some air!

cuffs
handcuffs
Example: don't let him to escape . slap the cuffs on him

de-nudulating
putting clothes on.
Example: could you hold the line? I'm just de-nudulating myself

dibbs
A set of clothing, often with accessories.
Example: Hey, Lauryn! Nice dibbs

duds
Clothing.
Example: With those duds, Alec is clearly one hip cat.

embare-assed
What happens when you take your clothes in a public place
Example: When I was changing in the bathroom stall, I became embare-assed

flopchki
Any type of sandal (usually of the pool and beach variety) that makes that slapping noise against your foot when you walk.
Example: My brother threw my new pink flopchki off the boat and now I have to walk around barefoot.

fly by the seat of one's pants
suddenly
Example: I have no idea how to do this but I'm just gonna fly by the seat of my pants

gear
clothes
Example: how much bucks should I pay for that gear?

give someone the boot
to fire someone from office
Example: after ten years of service, they gave me the boot

goody two-shoes
uptight and pretentious , arrogant
Example: don't be a goody two-shoes

hang onto your hat!
get ready to hear something
Example: you 're not going to believe what I have to tell you . hang onto your hat!

have one's hat off to someone
to respect someone
Example: my hat's off to your father

hit someone below the belt
to commit a contemptible or unfair act
Example: he stole my car . he hit me below the belt

hot under the collar
irritable and angry
Example: what's wrong with her? she seems hot under the collar

if the shoe fits , wear it
an affirmation of one's character trait
Example: I bought this beemer today . If the shoe fits wear it

in one's shoes
in one's situation
Example: what would you have done if you were in my shoes?

keep it under one's hat
keep it as a secret
Example: keep it under your hat and don't tell anyone

keep one's shirt on
be patient
Example: she will call you . keep your shirt on

lose one's shirt
to lose everything in life
Example: he lost his shirt when he went gambling

oldhat
old fashioned
Example: that style of hair is oldhat

rags
clothes
Example: just put on your rags and make it snappy!

shake in one's boots
to shake with fear
Example: when I saw the ghost , I started shaking in my boots

shake in ones boot
to shake with fear
Example: as soon as I saw the ghost , I shook in my boot

smarty pants
an intellectual who shows off
Example: your friend is a smarty pants.

stuffed shirt
uptight and pretentious
Example: he is a real stuffed shirt

sunday best
best clothes
Example: what's up man? You put on Sunday best

threads
clothes
Example: what a nice threads you 've bought!

wear more than one hat
to have more than one responsibility or position at work
Example: he wears more than on hat in his job

wear one's heart on one's sleeve
to be extremely compassionate
Example: she wears her heart on her sleeve

wear the pants in the family
to be the head of the family
Example: It sticks like a sore thumb who wears the pants in that family

wig out
to lose control of one's emotion
Example: he got angry and wig out

you bet your boots!
certainly
Example: did you lock the door? you bet your boots!

Color

beet red
to be extremely red from blushing , embarrassment
Example: he was so embarrassed he turned beet red

black as coal
extremely dark or evil
Example: Her heart is black as coal

black as the night
extremely dark
Example: My computer is always black as the night

blackball someone
to prevent someone from being hired or accepted to a specific group
Example: He can't find work because he was blackballed

blue
upset
Example That movie always make me blue

blue blood
opposite of bastard
Example: She said , I'm a blue blood

blue boys
police
Example: Watch out blue boys are coming

blue in the face
too tired
Example: I laughed until I was blue in the face

boys in blue
police
Example: He finally became a boys in blue

catch someone red-handed
to discover someone in the process of committing a dishonest act
Example: I know he 's guilty . I caught him red-handed

code Red
very popular person
Example: Jennifer Lopez in my opinion is a total Code red

county blues
Jail uniforms. Usually blue.
Example: Now that she's in prison she has to wear county blues.

give someone a black eye
to hit someone in the eye causing the surrounding are to become bruised
Example: I complaint about his manner and he gave me a black eye

gray area
vague stuff, uncertain issue
Example: That's really gray area. I can't get it

gray matter
intelligence
Example: I think he doesn't have any gray matter

green
amateur, novice
Example: I won't hire you. You are green

green-eyed monster
jealousy
Example: That's the green-eyed monster talking

green with envy
envious
Example: I'm green with envy of people that have those big houses

in the black
be in a good financial situation
Example: this year, we 're in the black

in the pink
be healthy
Example: You look like you 're in the pink today

in the red
in financial trouble
Example: This year , we 're in the red

look green around the gill
to look sick
Example: what's wrong with you ? you look green around the gill

men in blue
police
Example: Men in the blue arrested two people in connection with the robbery

no to have a red cent
not to have a single coin
Example: I can't lend you any money . I have no red cent

out of the blue
out of nowhere . suddenly
Example: the other driver appeared out of blue

paint the town red
to go partying
Example: I like to paint the town red now

pinky
one's little finger
Example: he always wears a ring on his pinky

purple passion
an intense passion
Example: I have a purple passion to become an actor

red
communist
Example: His friend is a red

red faced
embarrassed
Example: Did you see how red faced he was?

red hot
exceptional
Example: that movie is a red hot

red-letter day
important occasion
Example: This is a red-letter day in our community

redneck
bigot , prejudiced
Example: His father is a real redneck

roll out the red carpet for someone
to give someone first class treatment
Example: when my father comes to visit , we have to roll out the red carpet

see red
to be furious
Example: when I saw her with my ex boyfriend , I saw red!

swear up a blue streak
to swear , to curse
Example: She always swears up a blue streak

talk till one is blue in the face
to talk while being ignored .
Example: I talked to her till I was blue in the face

technicolor yawn
vomit , ralph
Example: whenever we go on a trip , my little sister make a technicolor yawn

the grass is always greener on the other side
Example: I 'd like to move to a small town . but I suppose the grass is always greener on the other side

tickled pink
excited , thrilled
Example: When I heard that I won the lottery , I was tickled pink

turn beet red
get angry
Example: When his mother discovered what jack had done , she turned beet red

what in blue blazes!?
exclamation of surprise and annoyance
Example: What in blue blazes boys?!

white as a ghost
extremely pale due to fear
Example: What's cooking man ? you look white as a ghost

white as a sheet
extremely pale due to fear
Example: He was white as a sheet

white bread
to be very unadventurous
Example: He 's so white bread

white lie
a trivial lie
Example: My friend says white lie whenever I see him

yellow
cowardly
Example: You 're not going to confront her? you are yellow

Crime

behind bars
in jail , in prison
Example: for a long he was behind bars

blow
cocaine
Example: police arrested two criminal with a lots of blow

can
prison, jail
Example: he was sentenced to six month in can

cooler
jail , prison
Example: Josh was in cooler when he kicked the
bucket

ex-con
someone who has spent time in jail
Example: one of his friend is a ex-con

ice
to kill someone
Example: If you tell Mom , I'll ice you

jack
to steal
Example: they broke into cars to steal the radios

joint
a prison, a jail
Example: his son is in a joint now because of
shoplifting .

yard bird
culprit , criminal
Example: in my vicinity there is no yard bird

Honest & dishonest
anjalistic
Innocent; trusts everybody, at times unassumingly.
Example: The girl anjalistically talked to the man,
who was years older than her, unaware of his flirting
with her.

at the up and up
honest
Example: He always is at the up and up with me

bag
to steal
Example: He never paid me back , so basically he ended up bagging a hundred dollars from me

blast
to strongly reprimand
Example: The committee blasted and censured him for his uncooperative attitude

cahoots
(in phrase **in cahoots**) in collusion; working together secretly
Example: In some soccer match they make cahoots

chat up
to tax somebody's mind
Example: He finally could chat up her mind

chiger
to lie.
Example: Don't chiger me, you mess.

clip
to cheat
Example: They got clipped out of their money

clocksucker
skive off from job
Example: What a clocksucker he is!

clown mounch
someone who bothers other by his acting
Example: Stop acting like clown mounch

con
to persuade someone to do something in order to
cheat them
Example: He was con by his girlfriend to steal his
father's car

creep
to backbite someone , to talk behind someone
Example: Have you heard, one of our coworkers is
creeping with the boss' wife.

cringent
Causing one to cringe.
Example: The way he smiles is cringent.

deceivious
Both deceitful and devious.
Example: I didn't trust him after seeing his
deceivious smile.

Deceptacon
A person suspected of being a liar, or untruthful.
Example: Don't trust Jimmy. I think he might be a
deceptacon

do a snow job on
to cajole someone
Example: He did a snow job on his family to get a
inheritance

egypped
to swindle
Example: I won the auction and sent the money but I was egypped when I did not receive the merchandise

express-hole
shoplifter
Example: he 's a express-hole

fife
to blatantly lie to someone, especially an absurd lie
Example: He said he had met the Pope at the Trekkie convention, but he was just fifing.

fizzake
Fake.
Example: that's a fizzake cheque

flatterpuss
copycat.
Example: Jane was just a flatterpuss when it came to Linda's elegant style.

flitigate
One who purposely breaks down the emotional state of another for her own amusement.
Example: Rhea was flitigating me yesterday, making nasty remarks about my personal life. Then she left just as I was about to cry.

get enroned
cheated out of money
Example: We are all about to get enroned

hanky panky
deception , monkeyshine
Example: with hankey-panky he could be a boss of the company .

hoofbeat
To flee someone you promised to aid, particularly in dire distress.
Example: He promised to help me with my term paper, but when it was time to write it, he did a hoofbeat.

hook
to steal
Example: They hooked all the gold in store

kissed up
to flatter
Example: He always kisses up to the teacher

knock over
to rob a bank
Example: They came to the bank , kill the boss and knocked over bank

lie like a rug
to tell enormous lies
Example: The guys lies like a rug

nab
to catch someone doing something wrong
Example: I was nabbed when i was trying to

on the level
honest, truthful
Example: he 's on the level with me when he wants to say something

rib
to tease someone in a friendly way
Example: he ribbed me and didn't tell the correct mark that I'd got

rip off
to cheat , rob , dishonest action
Example: The restaurant was ripped off

scam
a scheme to get money dishonestly
Example: There are lots of scam in internet

screw
to cheat or swindle someone
Example: She tried to screw him out of the tickets

sock
really honest guy
Example: Your friend is not sock with me

sucker
be deceived
Example: John is a real sucker

swept off ones feet
to be seduced
Example: He swept her off her feet as soon as they met

upfront
honest, open
Example: All of my friends are upfront with me

walked off
to stole
Example: Someone walked off my car

whopper
a "big" lie
Example: Her report is full of whoppers and misinformation

Dislike

clown-munch
A person that is stupid in your eyes, or someone that makes you angry.
Example: That driver behind me is a clown-munch.

crum
Something that you dislike
Example: That's so cheap looking , It's crum. I wouldn't be caught wearing it.

crumbler
someone who hates everything
Example: crumblers don't like to go to parties.

dilligaff
Short for Do I look like I care? When someone tells you something you are uninterested in, instead of saying I don't care
Example: Joe: nice weather today. Mary: dilligaff

disgroostifying
Very disgusting, often in a humorous way.
Example: When you burp like that, It's absolutely disgroostifying.

don't want to know
have no interest
Example: I don't want to know who did get married to?

edjaymic
disgusting, dirty, foul.
Example: I think Janet's underwear is edjaymic because it smells and it is really disgusting.

eerugh
offensive, disgusting, unrefined.
Example: eeurgh, this sandwich is nasty.

Fek
used to show disgust at something, or to describe something disgusting.
Example: that was the fekest thing I have ever seen

foily
Unpleasant; disgusting; bad. Possibly derived from foiled, as in Curses! Foiled again.
Example: Stay away from the spam quiche -- It's really foily.

gross
to be disgusting
Example: I'm not eating that , it looks gross

hate someone's guts
to hate somebody a lot
Example: I hate his guts . I don't like to talk to him anymore

not too keen
don't like
Example: I'm not too keen to come to your birthday party

yappy-ho-yap-yap
When you are not interested in hearing what the other person you are engaged in conversation with is saying, you then interrupt them with this word.
Example: A. And then I went to the-B: Yappy-ho-yap-yap.

yuck
disgusting
Example: yuck ! what is this stuff?

Drink

abbeverate
To feed a person a drink, to offer a drink, or provide a drink.
Example: I'm going to abbeverate our guests before they die of thirst.

alchitude
drunk
Example: He's got alchitude

ale-adote
wine
Example: It has been a real tough week. I think I
need a an ale-adote tonight

as clear as muddy water
obvious , noticeable , conspicuous
Example: That crime was a s clear as muddy water

barley pop
A beer.
Example: Hey, son, throw me another barley pop.

big drink
sea , ocean
Example: We flew over the big drink for an hour or
two

Blitzed
drunk
Example: Whenever you meet him , he is blitzed

booze
alcohol, liquor
Example: I can't get any more booze

down
to drink wine
Example: If I hadn't downed too much booze , I
would not have had this hallucinating

dressed in black label
To be drunk at a funeral
Example: I can't believe Jimmy showed up dressed
in black label. That little punk

drinkish
To be somewhat drunk, or buzzed.
Example: We went to the party and got drinkish enough to kiss each other publicly.

fine as wine
very handsome
Example: Your girlfriend is fine as wine man

flamming
Drunk.
Example: I was flamming last night.

off your face
to be very drunk
Example: you can't talk to the boss now . you are off your face now!

pissed
drunk
Example: After four glasses of wine , he was pissed

plastered
drunk
Example: He was plastered when i asked him to give me some bucks

shitfaced
very drunk
Example: He was shitfaced and couldn't talk to us

smashed
drunk
Example: After drinking too much wine , he was smashed

spifflicated
drunk
Example: The man was a little bit spifflicated

tipsy
slightly drunk
Example: Just by drinking one wine he got tipsy

vino
wine
Example: They usually buy vino

wrecked
very drunk
Example: John was wrecked when he talk to his ex girlfriend

Zizzy Ballooba
alcoholic drink.
Example: I have a terrible hangover. Had too many Zizzy Balloobas last night

zoodled
drunk
Example: She must be zoodled

Ear

all ears
very eager to hear
Example: when I was talking to my friend , she was all ears .

believe ones ears

to believe what you hear

Example: If you hear that news , you don't believe your ears!

bend one's ear

to talk to someone continually

Example: he bent my ear for an entire hour

blow it out one's ear

a contemptuous response to someone's annoying remark

Example: she blew it out my ear in front of bunch of people in party

chew someone ear off

to talk to someone for a long time

Example: he can really chew your ear off

ear duster

a talker

Example: he is an ear duster

ear to the ground

to pay attention the way things are going or to the way people feel

Example: you gotta ear to the ground and listen what I'm saying .

earbash

non-stop chatter

Example: Jane is a earbash . she could talk about an hour nonstop .

earful
large amount of unasked for advice or information
Example: I heard an earful of gossip today

Earsle
Ear.
Example: I heard it with my own earsle!

earvalanche
large mass of earwax or other ear debris suddenly and
unexpectedly falling from the ear
Example: I had an embarrassing earvalanche during
dinner, and several large pieces of wax fell into my
soup.

earworm
a song that repeats annoyingly in one's head
Example: when I was in subway , I heard a really
awful music and since then It's stucked in my mind
like a earworm

fall on deaf ears
to talk to someone who is not listening
Example: stop explaining . It's all falling on deaf
ears .

flea in ones ear
an idea or answer that is not welcomed
Example: Don't flea in your ears . I was not there at
all .

give somebody an earful
to punish somebody
Example: Because of talking behind me , I'm gonna
give him an earful

have ear for music
to have an aptitude for music
Example: he has an aptitude for music

lead an ear
listen to
Example: can you really lead an ear to music while you do your homework?

perk up ones ears
to catch ones attention
Example: It perked up my ears when I heard him mention my name

put a bug in ones ears
to warn someone
Example: I think the boss is going to be laying off the employees who are not working hard enough . I just want to put a bug in your ears

turn a deaf ear
to pretend not to hear
Example: he turned a deaf ear to me when I asked about my money

still wet behind your ears
Not having enough experience
Example: you are still wet behind your ears to work with computer .

Exclamation

ack
Exclamation used to indicate surprise, irritation, or disgust, often with one's own actions.
Example: Ack! I deleted my entire inbox!

chakos
Exclamation, when something surprises you.
Example: Chakos! This is the real stuff.

eekles
Exclamation, when something surprises you
Example: Eeekles! Look at that man dancing with the cheese.

fantabulous
to exclaim when something is very good/wonderful/pleasurable
Example: what a fantabulous pizza that was

for corn sake!
oh my goodness!
Example: for corn sake ! they will come again?

what in blue blazes!
a very crowded and busy situation
Example: what in blue blazes here!

yaggie
An expression to denote extreme happiness.
Example: No more math lessons. yaggie!

you got it !
I agree
Example: you got it! let's go there and live it up!

you said it !
I agree
Example: you said it! we will do that

Eye

acheye
The pain you feel in your eyes after looking at a screen for ages.
Example: after watching two hours movie , I got acheye .

all eyes
watching very closely
Example: she was looking at me in all eyes .

an eye for an eye
punishment equal to the harm which was done
Example : an eye for an eye .

angels rubbing my eyes
feeling really tired in eyes
Example: my stomach hurts and I've got angels rubbing my eyes

apple of ones eye
someone or something that ones like a lot
Example: you are apple of my eyes darling .

bat an eye
to show surprise , fear or interest
Example: she didn't bat an eye when I told her the news

believe ones eyes
to believe what one sees
Example: Don't believe your eyes whatever your hear

bird-watcher
eyeball
Example: he's a bird watcher .

blinkers
eyes
Example: as I opened my blinkers , guess who I saw?

bug an eye
To spy, or deliberately see something, especially when someone is curious.
Example: There is always someone bugging an eye on my PC monitor here at work.

bug eyed
having eyes that stick out
Example: did you notice her with bug eyed?

catch ones eye
to attract one's attention
Example: she caught my eyes in subway yesterday .

chippy chaser
to have rowing eyes
Example: in spite of being an old man , Jack's father is a chippy chaser

Crudbunny
The stuff that collects in the corner of your eye.
Example: Honey, you have a big crudbunny in your right eye

deuce
To poke someone in the eye with two fingers.
Example: Sometimes I wear a special face mask so that I can't be deuced.

eye candy
A gorgeous guy
Example: I saw your brother last night , he is pure eye candy

eye catcher
attractive person or thing
Example: she is a real eye catcher

eye for something
good taste
Example: he has an eye for painting

eye opener
something that wonder someone
Example: I don't know why they didn't come to party tonight . that's a eye opener

eye someone
to scrutinize someone with great interest
Example: when I first met her. she eyed me up and down

eyeball
to stare at someone or something
Example: stop eyeballing all the time .

eyeball to eyeball
very close to somebody and looking at them
Example: the protesters and police stood eyeball to
eyeball

eyelock
An unrecognizable foreign object in the road.
Example: Viewing some eyelocks may be an
unpleasant experience

eyes
sunglasses
Example: excuse me , how much dollar is this eyes?

eyes bigger than ones stomach
to be less hungry than one thought
I think I ordered too much food . I guess my eyes are
bigger than my stomach .

eyes in the back of ones head
ability to know what happens when one's back is
turned
Example: you should have eyes in the back of your
head until I come back .

eyes pop out
one is very surprised
Example: my eyes popped out when I saw John is
her car

eyesore
something that is offensive to look at
Example: that painting is an eyesore

eyewash
nonsense
Example: all you are trying to say is eyewash .

four-eyes
condescending term who wears glasses
Example: hey four eyes . what's up?

give ones eyetooth for something
to risk anything in order to obtain something
Example: I'd give my eyethooth to look like her

give someone a black eye
to bruise someone's eye by hitting it
Example: where did you get that black eye?

make goo-goo eyes at someone
to look at somebody in lovely way
Example: you must have seen her that was making goo-goo eyes at me .

green eyed monster
jealously
Example: that is jealously talking

have an eye for
to be able to judge correctly
Example: he has an eye for going to gym .

have eyes only for
to see or want nothing else , give all one's attention .
Example: when he came to my house , he had eyes only for my laptop

hit between the eyes
to make a strong impression on
Example: she was hit between the eyes by the common sense views of her grandparents .

in a pig's eye
nonsense
Example: she told me she speaks ten languages . in a pig's eye!

in ones minds eye
in one's imagination
Example: she is in my minds eye forever .

keep an eye on someone
to watch over someone
Example: I have to stay here and keep and eye on my little brother .

keep one's eyes peeled
to stay alert
Example: keep your eyes peeled

lamps
the eyes
Example: his lamps are closed . he's asleep or dead .

make eyes at
try to attract someone
Example: I was in shopping mall that two girls made eyes at me

peepers
eyes
Example: grandma , you have such big peepers

see eye to eye
to be in agreement with someone
Example: we always see eye to eye

shuteye
sleep
Example: I need to get some shuteye

specs
eyeglasses
Example: where did you buy that specs?

to the naked eye
as it seen , apparently
Example: to the naked eye , you are losing some
weight

Face

arse-about-face
something that is in a mess or crooked
Example: that car is a arse about face

Barbofski
huge mustaches or people that wear them.
Example: do you know who the boss is? Yeah the
man with barbofski mustache

button one's lip
to stop talking
Example: would you please button your lips .
because I'm thinking

by the skin of one's teeth
barely
Example: I passed the test by the skin of my teeth

chain smoker
a person who smoke all the time frequently .
Example: my uncle is a chain smoker

cheeky
to be disrespectful
Example: stop being so cheeky

chickindeenis
Any part of one's body.
Example: Hey, get your chickindeenis over here.

china
tooth
Example: I cant eat anything . I have a pain in my china

chive
Something stuck between your teeth
Example: Do you have a toothpick? I think I have a chive

crustache
a mustache that doesn't have enough hair and is 'crusty'
Example: Eww that guy has such a crustache..Shave!

face card
important guy
Example: he 's a face card

ivories
tooth
Example: I have a pain in my ivories .

lip
disrespectful talk
Example: I don 't want any more lip out of you !

long in the tooth
to be old
Example: our dog is getting long in the tooth

map
face
Example: Cal hid his map in his hands .

pay someone lip service
to downgrade the importance of something that which comes from the mouth and not the heart
Example: what I'm saying is true . I'm not just paying you lip service

sweet tooth
someone who loves sweet
Example: my little brother is a sweet tooth .

talk till one is blue in the face
to talk a lot until get bored
Example: he talked till his is blue in the face .

watch your mouth
be careful what your saying
Example: Example

Feel

Abyssicaletphedence
An endless nothingness of boredom.
Example: James sat in abyssicaletphedence during class

all flurbudgeoned
agitated and confused.
Example: I got all flurbudgeoned when Mike unexpectedly asked me out.

all in
too tired
Example: she was all in when came to home

allymcbealing
Talking to oneself aloud and having hallucinations.
Example: Oh, my God, I'm allymcbealing!

angels rubbing my eyes
feel really tired
Example: jack, my stomach hurts and I've got angels rubbing my eyes.

Antipathic
Against feeling, heartless.
Example: He was antipathic to her.

antsy
nervous
Example: my teacher always is so antsy

ape
very angry
Example: When my parents saw my report card, they went ape

basket case
nervous , angry
Example: hey , you look basket case today , what s up?

beat
tired, exhausted, weary
Example: she had been up all night with the baby and was really beat

bent out of shape
to become angry
Example: she is going to get all bent out of shape

blown away
to upset someone
Example: she always make me blown away

bummed
depressed
Example: what's the matter with you man , you are too bummed today

bummed out
upset
Example: why are u bummed out again

bushed
too tired
Example: she is just bushed

chirpacious
overly cheerful.
Example: She was so chirpacious . It got on my nerves

corall'd
feel generally crappy or over tired.
Example: I am feeling so corall'd after last night

deepdish
look perplexed or overwhelmed by some problem
Example: He is acting so strange, it makes you wonder what his deepdish is all about.

dredger
Something or someone that is tedious or boring.
Example: People stopped hanging out with Greg because listening to his long stories about statistics was a real dredger.

dry baulk
A feeling of nausea. An urge to vomit, but checked by a dry gagging or choking of the throat.
Example: The smell was bad enough to give you the dry baulk

eat somebody
to be extremely angry with said person, to the point of having the desire to kill and eat him or her.
Example: After I ambushed him with snowballs, I thought he was going to eat me. He was taking it the wrong way.

eholay
a term to be used when you are frustrated.
Example: you just get so eholay , what's wrong?

ello-ell
LOL--meaning laughing out loud.
Example: I'm ello-ell.

Emoticate
To communicate with someone using only emotions.
Example: When I emoticate with my girlfriend she knows exactly what's on my mind.

equidelirium
state of being delirium
Example: Am I really equidelirius?

equinosity
Horse sense; common sense
Example: He is a man of great equinosity.

exhausticated
when you are extremely tired
Example: I can't go out tonight, I am too exhausticated

fadated
Having a lack of energy, feeling tired.
Example: I just dug up the backyard, so I'm now feeling pretty fadated

faintified
Feeling faint or dizzy.
Example: I feel faintified.

faschnickered
Very tired.
Example: She was so faschnickered she couldn't walk

fed up
depressed
Example: you look a bit fed up

feel blah
feel terrible
Example: I felt blah when I saw him in the gym

feel under the weather
feel sick
Example: today our teacher feel under the weather guys! what's the matter with him?

flabbergammered
To be so astonished that you stammer.
Example: Marie was flabbergammered when she spotted John exiting that hotel with her best friend. . .

flap
panic
Example: I was flap when I saw my daddy in school

flip out
very upset
Example: I was flip out since i got my exam's result

florama

if you feel really weird you don't know what to do.
You don't know what will happen and you see
everything blurry

Example: As I woke up one day I was in a deep
florama

fly off the handle

to become suddenly angry

Example: she flied off the handle and said nonsense
to me

freak

react very emotionally

Example: why you got freak man !

freak someone out

make somebody very upset

Example: she always freak me out when I tell her to
hang out

freaked

upset

Example: she was rather freaked last night in party

go ape

to become angry suddenly

Example: my dad went ape when he saw my mark

have good vibes

feel good about something

Example: I have good vibes about it . don't worry

huffy
angry
Example: when she refused him to talk , he got huffy

jumpy
anxious, uneasy, on edge
Example: I was so jumpy until she called

knackered
very tired, exhausted
Example: I can't go out tonight , I'm knackered

on pins and needles
excited and nervous waiting for somebody
Example: I was on pins and needles waiting for him
to arrive

pooped
very tired, exhausted
Example: you can't talk to him . he is pooped

sneak suspicion
feel
Example: what's your sneak suspicion about coming
here?

someone is not ones self
being sad
Example: your not your self man , what's happened?

steamed up
become angry
Example: mom , come here , daddy is steamed up
again!

stressed out
nervous
Example: It seems he's going to be stressed out

sweat bullets
be extremely nervous or anxious
Example: I started sweating bullets because I knew I failed my exam

tear jerker
sad emotional film
Example: she is dying bit of a tear jerker

ticked off
angry
Example: that girl really ticks me off

unglued
upset
Example: now you shouldn't get all unglued

upbeat
bright, cheerful
Example: I was upbeat when i saw my exam's result

uptight
worried , anxious
Example: you look uptight . tell me what's wrong?

Z-Monster
tiredness so excessive you can't keep your eyes open
Example: That Z-Monster is beating me down

zonked out
to become very tired
Example: the long hike up the mountain zonked out us

Food

achecanantooch
To eat foreign food.
Example: I'm hungry. Let's achecanantooch all night!

antiscurvies
Green vegetables
Example: No desert until you eat your antiscurvies.

as easy as ducky soup
easy
Example: this match is as easy as ducky soup for me

as easy as pie
easy to do
Example: this is going to be as easy as pie

baloney
nonsense
Example the man said , your talking baloney

bean counter
accountant
Example my cousin is a bean counter

bean time
time for serving lunch
Example hey , you guys, It's a bean time

beef
a conflict with someone; a complaint against someone
Example: he made a beef with me at the police office

beefy
muscular
Example: her boyfriend is so beefy

big cheese
the boss
Example: he 's the big cheese here

big drink
sea , ocean
Example: these mysterious creatures live at the bottom of the big drink

big enchilada
the boss
Example: who is the big enchilada here?

blood
ketchup
Example: give me the blood please

bread and butter
a persons live hood or main source of income
Example: I don't bread and butter anymore . I've got everything here

bread winner
the member of the family who supports the family
Example: he is the bread winner of the family

bring home bacon
earn money for food
Example: there was no one to bring home bacon

buns
buttocks
Example: He has a pain in his buns

cake and pie
So easy as to be laughable, a piece of cake and easy as pie combined
Example: Doing graphics on a Macintosh? Cake and pie!

cakehead
Someone who is not very bright.
Example: That cakehead just ran that red light.

cakewalk
Easily done, same as a piece of cake.
Example: Our calculus test was cakewalk.

can of corn
Really corny.
Example: Those red polka dot shoes? They deserve a can of corn

Chawny

pertaining to food. unpalatable in both flavor and tastes

Example: Ugh! I am never staying at Eugene's house again. His mom serves up chawny pig-slop

cheese

vomit

Example: stop the car . I wanna cheese!

To be happy and not worry

Example: Don't cry. Life is short, so just be chees

cheese and rice

Jesus Christ.

Example: Cheese and rice! Would you look at that?

cheese eater

a person who says the news to each other

Example: you can't tell anything to her . she 's a cheese eater.

cheese wagon

a large, yellow, American school bus.

Example: Until I can afford a Camaro I have to take the cheese wagon to school.

cheesed

To be extremely angry with someone or something

Example: That guy hit your car? I'd be cheesed!

cheesy

cheap and lacking in taste

Example: Don't wear this shirt . look likes cheesy to you

cheesyfeet
bad smell of a feet
Example : hey yo! Go and take off your socks . they smell cheesyfeet

chevybread
Bread that is hard and old.
Example: This sandwich has ChevyBread Yuck!

chew out
to reprimand
Example: John is in with boss getting chewed out now

chew someone out
to scold someone
Example: he really chewed me out !

Chive scan
The practice of examining your date's teeth after a meal to make sure there are no lingering food particles. Can be abbreviated "CS."
Example: Can you run a chive scan, make sure I'm clear?

chocolate teapot
Something that is useless for what it is designed.
Example: I know it looks good, but it doesn't work at all. It's about as useful as a chocolate teapot

chomley
a contraction of chamomile tea.
Example: Would you like a cup of chomley?

chomps
any type of food
Example: I'm hungry. I'm gonna get me some chomps

chow
food, grub
Example: That's a really great chow

chow down
to eat food
Example: I can't wait to chow down

city juice
Water from the tap.
Example: Could I get a glass of city juice? asked the man of the waitress.

clam up
to stop talking
Example: we tried to get him to confess but he just clammed up

coffee break
recess , break time
Example: Excuse me master . how much coffee break we have?

cook something up
to prepare something
Example: we have a guest tonight . we gotta cook food up

cook with gas
to perform extremely well
Example: you are cooking with gas! bravo!

cool beans
cool stuff.
Example: Cool beans garbanzo!

couch potato
lazy guy
Example: get up and do some exercise couch potato

cut the cheese
fart
Example: who cut the cheese?

cut the mustard
to become successful
Example: the boss fired her . because he couldn't cut the mustard

delicatessian
Exceptionally delicious junk food.
Example: That pizza was a delicatessian delight.

dibble
a little bit of something, as in food or drink
Example: How big of a piece of cake do you want? Just a dibble

don't put all your eggs in one basket
don't destroy all your chances that you have
Example: don't put all your eggs in one basket

Dr pepper
Coca Cola
Example: Do you want a drink? Yeah. What kind?
Dr Pepper

easy as pie
extremely easy
Example: It's easy as pie

eat high off the hog
to eat expensive foods
Example: I ate at Nancy 's house last night. they
really eat high off the hog

eat humble pie
to say sorry , excuse me
Example: Ok , I eat humble pie . Leave me alone!

eat ones cake and have it
use and spend something and still keep it
Example: you eat your cake and have it!?

eats
a slang word for food of any kind.
Example: I'm hungry--let's go down town and get
some eats

egg sucker
sycophant
Example: you 're such a egg sucker

egghead
a highly-educated intellectual
Example: he's a egghead in this town

eggsucker
sycophant
Example: we have lots of eggsucker in class

feach
potato
Example: I would like a baked feach

feed one's face
to eat
Example: I'm hungry . I wanna feed my face now

fine as wine
attractive , handsome
Example: that guy is fine as wine . don't you like talk to him?

Foo-Foo food
Chinese food
Example: I feel like foo-foo food tonight, how about you?

Foodage
Slang for food
Example: I'm going down to the shops to pick up some foodage

freeze one's buns off
very cold
Example: we froze our buns off this winter

fudge it
to make a booboo
Example: he fudged it again in his sister's wedding

fudge!
damn it
Example: fudge it man ! we lose again

grub
food
Example: I'm hungry . Let's go and have some grubs to eat

half baked
not a good idea
Example: I think your idea is half baked

ham
a performer
Example: in the future I want to be a ham

ham it up
to overact
Example: he 's really hamming it up

happy as a clam
very happy
Example: the little boy was happy as a clam

have a bun in the oven
to be pregnant
Example: I hear you have a bun in the oven

have one's goose cooked
to be in big trouble
Example: if my mother sees us , our goose is gonna be cooked

in a stew
upset
Example: Don't get your self in a stew about her

in the chips
rich , wealthy
Example: he has got three beemer . he is in the chips

instafood
food that can be prepared in 5 minutes or less
Example: mom , what do we have today for lunch ?
instafood

keep egging
continue urging & insisting
Example: I kept egging my father to buy me a laptop

knuckle sandwich
to punch somebody
Example: If you don't stop bothering me , I'm gonna
give you a knuckle sandwich

limp as a noodle
totally droopy
Example: when I came back from school , I was limp
as a noodle

lose ones cookies
to have vomit
Example: after drinking too much booze he lost his
cookies .

noodle
head or brain
Example: use your noodle and answer the easy
question silly

noodle around

to play around , horse around

Example: you are just noodling around . stop it!

nut

crazy

Example: the woman said , who are you , some kind of a nut?

nutty as a fruit cake

crazy

Example: after seeing the dead body , she became nutty as a fruit cake

off one's noodle

crazy

Example: you 're off your noodle!

piece of cake

easy

Example: the exam was a piece of cake for him

put on the feed bag

to eat

Example: Let 's go put out on the feed bag

sammich

Sandwich.

Example: I'm gonna eat me a sammich.

sand

sugar

Example: give me a sand please

sandwiched
trapped between two things
Example: I got sandwiched between the elevetor's
door

sarnie
sandwich
Example: my kids always eat sarnie for lunch

sell like hotcakes
to sell well
Example: his book are selling like hotcakes

smart cookie
to be smart and clever
Example: he is the smart cookie in our class

spoon feed someone
to explain something slowly
Example: he is so slow . you have to spoon feed him

spud
potato
Example: I ate spud with yogurt yesterday night

sugar
term of endearment
Example: where are you going sugar?

sugar daddy
godfather , man who provides money to the one he
keeps
Example: that must be her sugar daddy

sweet as sugar
very lovable
Example: he is so sweet as sugar

sweetie-pie
term of endearment
Example: Hi sweet-pie!

that's the way the cookie crumbles
that is just how things are
Example: that's the way the cookie crumbles . what you gonna do ?

the best thing since sliced bread
the very best , fantastic
Example: This car is the best thing since sliced bread

the whole enchilada
the entire matter
Example: and that ended our vacation . that's the whole enchilada

toss one's cookies
to vomit
Example: stop the car . I need to toss my cookies

tough cookie
strict person
Example: you are so tough cookie . did you know that?

veggie
vegetarian
Example : my parents are veggie

wake up and smell the coffee
to become aware
Example: you trusted him? wake up and smell the coffee!

wet noodle
one who exudes depression or sadness
Example: I don't want invite him . he 's wet noodle

what's cookin?
what's up?
Example: what's cookin man?

whip up
to make food ready
Example: whip up . we are coming to home now

za
The proper show form for pizza.
Example: Martha and I went out and grabbed some za.

Foot & Leg

back on one's feet
to recover , getting better from sickness or trouble
Example: our teacher was back on her feet shortly after she had her accident .

bad wheel
Injured or sore foot or ankle
Example: You look like you're limping a little. Bad wheel?

beat feet
to leave the scene in a hurry
Example: you can't beat feet now! It's not finished yet!

boot-leged
kicked
Example: Ouch! You just boot-leged me in the shin

bootleg
not right or not true
Example: What she said was so bootleg

break a leg
to say good luck to actors
Example: break a leg John!

cold feet
timid guy
Example: just when I was about to ask him for a raise I got cold feet

drag ones feet
to act slowly or reluctantly
Example: our company is dragging their feet in making a decision to hire new workers .

erthroitrageelatunny
The area between your big toe and the second biggest toe.
Example: I cut my erthroitrageelatunny

feet of clay
a hidden fault or weakness in a respected person
Example: the new prime minister has feet of clay and may not last very long in his new position .

feet on the ground
an understanding of what can be done , sensible ideas
Example: he has feet on the ground . he knows what to do in difficult situation .

foot the bill
to pay the bill
Example: I didn't have to pay anything . he said he would foot the entire bill

footloose
to be able to do anything one desires in ones life without any restrictions
Example: now that he's divorced , he's footloose

get a foot in the door
to take the first step in attaining a goal
Example you didn't get the job yet , but at least it's a foot in the door

get back on ones feet
to reestablish oneself after a failure
Example: after he lost his job , it took him a while to get back on his feet

get off on the wrong foot
to begin a friendship badly
Example we got off on the wrong foot , but we are friends

get one's feet wet
to become familiar with a situation or someone
Example: I don't really know what my job entails . I'm still getting my feet wet .

get under one's feet
to get in someone's way
Example she always gets under my feet

hail on foot
to run
Example so i hailed on foot to catch the bus

have a hollow leg
said of someone with a huge appetite
Example: I don 't know how he can eat so much . he must have a hollow leg

hotfoot it
to hurry
Example the movie starts in five minutes ! we'd better hotfoot it over to the theater

keep a stiff upper lip
to keep one's emotions under control
Example: don't worry , just keep a stiff upper lip .

kick up ones heels
to have a good time
Example: we kicked up our heels last night and had a great time at the party .

nock someone off their feet
surprise or shock someone so much that they don't know what to do
Example: he knocked him off their feet when he knew that he won the lottery .

land on ones feet
to come cut of a bad situation successfully
Example: I was able to land on my feet even through our company had recently gone bankrupt

leadfoot
to have a tendency to drive fast as if his/her foot were as heavy as lead on the accelerator
Example I don't like driving with him . he has a real lead foot

leg it
to walk
Example: let 's leg it to work today

let the grass grow under ones feet
to waste time
Example: don't let the grass grow under your feet and go to talk to her .

lily-livered
to be cowardly
Example: I've never met anyone so lily-livered

not to have a leg to stand on
not to have any justification for something
Example: I don't have a leg to stand on now .

on ones feet
to recover , getting better from sickness or trouble
Example: our teacher was back on her feet shortly after she had her accident .

on ones last leg
near the end , falling
Example: your car is on its last leg . you need to buy new one .

one foot in the grave
close to death
Example the poor man has one foot in the grave

ones foot down
to forbid
Example I have to put my foot down on that

pull ones leg
to fool someone
Example: are you trying to pull my leg?

put ones foot down
to object strongly , take firm action
Example: my sister finally out her foot down and stopped paying for the gas for her mother's car .

set foot
to enter somewhere
Example he sat foot in the club

shake a leg
to hurry up
Example: we 'd better shake a leg if we don 't want to be late

shoot off one's mouth
to say whatever comes to one's mind
Example: think a little before you go shooting off your mouth

stand on ones own two feet
to be self reliant
Example she has to learn to stand on her own two feet

stretch one's leg
to move around after having been motionless for a long period
Example: I'm going outside to stretch my legs

sweep off ones feet
to be seduced
Example: he swept her off her feet as soon as they met .

tail between one legs
state of feeling beaten . ashamed or very obedient as after a scolding or a whipping
Example: the salesman forced to leave the office with his tail between his legs after
he admitted telling a lie about his sales figures

throw ones self at someone's feet
to succumb to someone completely . to give up
Example he threw himself at her feet after walking about 2 hours .

wait on hand and foot
to do everything for someone
Example: I always wait hand and foot on my sister when she comes to visit me .

walk on one's heels
to walk too closely to someone
Example: stop walking on my heels!

wrong foot
untrustworthy friend
Example: all of his friends are wrong foot

Fruit

apple polisher
sycophant
Example: doesn't the wimpy apple polisher know how stupid he looks

as American as apple pie
a person whose born in USA
Example: my cousin is as American as apple pie

as cool as cucumber
very calm and relaxed
Example: he tried to stay as cool as a cucumber

banana oil
nonsense
Example: that is the ridiculous banana oil I have ever heard

bean town
Boston
Example: I like to live in bean town

beanbrain
idiot
Example :he is such a bean brain

beans about something
not to know anything about something
Example: I don't know beans about computers

beet red
to be very red from embarrassment
Example: she was so embarrassed she turned beet red

bowl of a cherries
to be wonderful
Example: life is not always a bowl of cherries

cherry
Original slang to mean a virgin, but now more
commonly used to describe something in pristine
condition.
Example: My Dad's 1970 Oldsmobile 442 is cherry.

compare apples and oranges
to compare two things that simply cannot be
compared
Example: That's awful , now your comparing apples
and oranges

cool as a cucumber
to be calm and composed
Example: although he 's guilty of the crime , he sure is cool as a cucumber

cornball
ridiculous
Example: where did you buy that cornball hat?

corny
old fashioned
Example: the movie was so corny

couch potato
a person who spends a great deal of their leisure time watching television. television addict
Example: she is a real couch potato

dangle a carrot in front of someone
to tempt someone with an unobtainable offer
Example the boss told me if i work well , he will increase my salary . but I think he is dangling a carrot in front of me

Ernie Orange
The color girls and guys get when they overtan or use self-tanning cream where the color does not look right. Named after the Sesame Street character of the same color.
Example: Suzanne looks Ernie orange today

for corn sake!
oh my goodness
Example: he said for corn sake!

fruitcake
an insane person , lunatic
Example: what a fruitcake he is

go banana
go crazy
Example: when my father saw the bills , he went banana

go bananas
get angry
Example: when my father saw the phone bill , he went banana

hen fruit
egg
Example: my mom called me and say whenever you wanted to come home buy me some hen fruits

hot potato
anything that is considered to be potentially dangerous or volatile
Example: this situation is real hot potato

how do you like them apples?
what do you think of that
Example: how do you like them apples? party or club?

in a pickle
to get in a difficult situation
Example: they were certainly in a pickle

lemon
worthless merchandise
Example: that car is real lemon

peach of a something
to be great
Example: she is a peach of a teacher

peachy
to be terrific , excellent
Example: that's really peachy book

pumpkin
sweetheart , honey
Example: hi pumpkin , what's up?

rotten apple
bad guy
Example: Jane is a real rotten apple

small potatoes
unimportant stuff
Example: that's small potatoes compared to the real
problem

sprout
young person
Example: he may be a sprout right now , but give
him a few more years

the apple of ones eyes
to love somebody a lot
Example: whenever we go to my grandpa's house ,
he tells me you 're the apple of my eyes

the big apple
nick name for New York
Example: where do you live man ? in the big apple

tomato
girl
Example: look at that tomato is coming here!

top banana
boss , leader
Example: she is the top banana in this company

wrinkled as a prune
to be very wrinkled
Example: my shirt is wrinkled as a prune

Good & bad quality

a dead loss
useless
Example: I'm afraid the new secretary is a dead loss

A1
very good
Example: that was a real A1 exam

absoludacris
Something absolutely ludicrous
Example: Drugs are bad and drugs are absoludacris.

absoludicrous
The peak of ridiculousness. absolutely ludicrous.
Example: Look! That guy has blue hair. How
absoludicrous

absopositively
Absolutely and positively combined.
Example: I am absopositively sure that Milton likes you

ace
take a good mark in exam
Example: I really aced that test

acklapootis
Cool, awesome, etc.
Example: Angelina Jolie is one acklapootis babe

adipolli
Superb, fantastic.
Example: The stage show was adipolli.

all system are go
every thing is ok
Example: Hey man now all system are go

amuzimatistical
amazing
Example: That track by method man was straight up amuzimatistical.

awesome
wonderful
Example: you own that gorgeous car ? awesome

aws
splendid , wonderful
Example: All the Hollywood actors are aws

bad
great , awesome
Example: that car is bad man!

bangin
very good
Example: That shirt is bangin'.

blast
a great time .
Example: "We had a blast at the Prom".

bomb
bad thing (theater , television , movies ...)
Example: that show was a real bomb

boombox
worthless thing
Example: that car you've got is boombox

Boss
A great or cool thing.
Example: The Beach Boys new record is really boss

bugger up
to ruin, spoil, mess up
Example: I bugger up in front of my boss today

bummer
bad experience
Example: Don't talk about it near me . It's such a bummer

calamatastrophy
Worse than a calamity but not quite a catastrophe.
Example: There was a calamatastrophy involving 23 cars on the freeway last night

chez-monkey
a nice way of saying something is cheesy, cheap, or poorly made.
Example: Did you see Linda's new rug? It is very chezmoid don't you think?

classy
high class
Example: classy , It will cost you a packet

cling cling
very clean area
Example: how did you clean your room? it's cling cling!

concrete
very good
Example: He told me , your ideas are not concrete

cooda
Fantastic, brilliant, awesome
Example: The pseudocictionary is cooda

coolie doolies
an alternative way of saying cool, yet more sytlish
Example: we wanna go to party tonight ? Coolie doolies

coolrunnings
everything is good or couldn't be better.
Example: How's it going? Coolrunnings!

corvus
Excellent, cool
Example: That is just corvus.

cugus
junk thing
Example: get rid of the cugus

da bomb
excellent, extremely good
Example: the movie I watched in channel 2 was da bomb

dandy
nifty; spiffy , good
Example: Have a dandy day.

dank
when referring to something really cool or nice
Example: Damn that car! . the new brand of beemer is a dank

diggidy-swizz
a way to say something was truly cool, great, or exciting.
Example: Man, did you see that girl? She was the diggidy-swizz!

dillyun
top, best, awesome, supremely excellent.
Example: Which models would you rate dillyun?

dussimo
Very bad.
Example: any Akon song is dussimo.

edjaymic
Disgusting, dirty, foul.
Example: I think Janet's underwear is edjaymic because it smells and it is really disgusting

el dussey
Very good or totally awesome.
Example: This website is el dussey. My Spanish word corruptions are totally el dussey

elegalorious
Elegant and glorious.
Example: The pie you made was elegalorious.

Eskimofo
A terrible cold thing. It may be a person, place, or thing.
Example: This winter has been such an eskimofo

eupulchrous
Truly, exceptionally beautiful.
Example: Check out that eupulchrous babe coming down the hall

expoobident
Extraordinary, phenomenal, wonderful.
Example: that party was expoobident

extra napkins

Something so good that you need extra napkins to clean up your drool.

Example: I needed extra napkins after seeing the new IPod

fab

fabulous , wonderful

Example: that was a fab beemer I've ever seen!

fancicus rex

Very cool, awesome.

Example: Your house is fancicus rex!

fancy shmancy

fancy and appealing

Example: hey look at that girl . she 's fancy shmancy

fandabidosy

Fantastic.

Example: We're having pancakes for breakfast? . fandabidosy

far out

great

Example: this new mercedes is far out

fierce

Cool.

Example: Her party was fierce.

fire

Very cool or the best; something that is very pleasing.

Example: That party was fire

fizabulizmous
Fabulous.
Example: That concert was absolutely fizabulizmous.

flint
High quality.
Example: That car is flint.

floss
showing off in front of people
Example: she 's walking and flossing in front of people

fly
cool
Example: that's a fly suit

for kicks
for fun
Example: we just did it for kicks

funky
bad smell of something
Example: what's that funky smell?

garbage
something of very poor quality
Example: this is a most garbage movie that I've ever seen

gear
excellent
Example: his music is really gear

good for nothing
something that worth nothing
Example: Jack never is useful for his parent . he 's
good for nothing

good Sense a yuma
good sense of humor
Example: he 's got a good sense a Yuma

good time charley
optimistic person
Example: good time charley and call her

groovy
excellent
Example: that's a nice groovy shirt . where did you
get it?

grubby
unclean
Example: oh , you gotta wash the car . It's become
grubby

grungy
dirty
Example: I was working in my office with a grungy
suit

gunner
good student in class
Example: Josh is a gunner in our class

hood
a neighborhood, especially in a poor, urban area
Example: he lives in a hood of city

hunky-dory
good, fine, going well
Example: every thing is hunkey dory . don't worry dude

ill
good, excellent
Example: wow man ! what a ill Audio !

kewl
cool! , excellent!
Example: you have a nice job . kewl!

kick
excellent , fun
Example: the is in kick condition .

killer
excellent, awesome, outstanding
Example: this color is a killer for this wall

loose ones cookies
vomit
Example: he was nervous that he was going to lose his cookies

louse up
to spoil something or make it fail
Example: he 's clumsy . he always louses up everything

mickey mouse
worthless
Example: it's really mickey mouse if you wanna do this job

mind boggling
amazing
Example: It's pretty mind boggling how much top athletes get paid .

muck up
to ruin something, or do it very badly
Example: he mucked up in his job and got fired quickly by his big enchilada

neat
good
Example: thanks mom . that was a neat soup

nice shmice
very nice
Example: you new car is nice shmice

one off
unique , exclusive
Example: he is a one off teacher in this school

outta slight
awesome , fantastic
Example: have you seen his new laptop? That's outta slight!

phat
excellent, wonderful, great
Example: becoming a father was the most phat experience of my life .

posh
high class
Example: last year I went to a posh hotel in LA .

ritzy
luxurious, high-class, expensive
Example: they had a ritzy wedding .

smashing
wonderful
Example: look at that smashing car over there!

stick as a dog
has a fever
Example: I'm stick as a dog . I can't hang out with you today

terrific
perfect , wonderful
Example: yesterday was a terrific day for me . I could pass the driving test .

tip top
excellent
Example: that was a tip top car that I ever had

trendy
fashionable
Example: the read head with trendy clothes

wacky
odd , eccentric
Example: he looks wacky today

Zeng
good or excellent.
Example: How was last night? Zeng!

zuzzy
a word used to describe something really, really bad.
Example: Your clothes look really zuzzy

Hair

anime-hair
extreme case of bed head in which hair defies gravity
and all known normal shape, similar to anime cartoon
characters.
Example: Stan woke up again with anime hair and
headed for the shower immediately.

blood nut
a person with excessive red- or ginger-colored hair.
Example: Q: Do you think her hair color's natural. A.
Sure, she's a blood nut

blue hairs
old people, especially women.
Example: How do you get 100 blue hairs to swear at
the same time? Yell BINGO!

chia pet
Someone with short, curly, frizzy chia pet hair. From
Chia pet.
Example: He's all right, but a bit of a chia pet

desperadoo
the kind of hair like ponytail
Example: he has a desperado in all his photo .

devon
bald, having no or little hair
Example: these days most people around the world are becoming devon

emerson
bald, hairless
Example: One of the best examples of an emerson is Yul Brynner

follicotomy
The result of a bad haircut.
Example: She cut way too short, so I now have a follicotomy

foomp
noun. a hairstyle that is trying to be a pompadour, but only succeeds in pushing all the hair on the head forward
Example: That's quite a foomp you have going on there today, Bob

hair raising
frightening
Example: what a hair raising story !

hairy
dangerous
Example: that must have been hairy !

let one's hair down
to relax and abandon all pretense
Example she finally let her hair down in front of us

Zazzera

Hair on the back of a person's neck.

Example: Can you please come here and trim my zazzera?

Hand

all thumbs

clumsy person

Example: you are all thumbs .

pay arm and a leg

to pay a very high price for something that is worthless

Example: I think I've paid arm and a leg for this car .

at hand

pressing , important

Example: what's the issue at hand ?

bite the hand that feeds one

to reply kindness with wrong

Example: my cousin is biting the hand that feeds her if he keeps abusing the help that his parents are giving her .

burn ones fingers

learn caution through an unpleasant experience

Example: I burn my finger to give him a hand again .

butterfingers

clumsy

Example: he is such a butterfingers . he dropped his papers

byhandual

using both hands with equal ease. Ambidextrous.
Example: Leonardo DaVinci was byhandual

dirty ones hands

to hurt one's character or good name
Example: the politician dirtied his hands when he
became involved in the questionable land deals .

finger in the dog's eye

Like having one's finger on the pulse, only
misguided.
Example: Those TV people really have the finger in
the dog's eye of public opinion. They don't know
anything.

give ones right arm

to give something of great value
Example: I won't give him right arm .

give someone a hand

to help someone
Example: I gave my friend a hand moving into his
apartment

give someone elbow room

to give someone space
Example: I can hardly move . give me some elbow
room

give someone the finger

to show somebody your thumb
Example: when I was in the bus , she gave me the
finger

glad hand
a friendly handshake , a warm greeting
Example: the politician spent all day glad handing the crowd at the shopping center .

grease ones palm
to pay a person for something done or given dishonestly
Example: we had to grease the palm of the customs agent at the border to get our goods in to the country .

hand
to give
Example: hand it to me right now !

hand it to someone
said in admiration of someone
Example : I've got to hand It to you

handout
offering , charity
Example: Although he doesn't have any money , he refuses to accept handouts

hands down
without exception .
Example: I think it's the best movie hands down

handy
useful
Example: your device was very handy , saving me a lot of time .

high handed

bossy , depending on force rather than what is right
Example: he took a high handed approach to the
negotiation and in the end he was not successful

in hand

under the control
Example: you can buy slanguage book . Its in hand
now

itching palm

a wish for money , greed
Example: the police officer had an itching palm and
took much money from criminals

know something like the back of ones hand

to know something extremely well .
Example: I know this city like the back of my hand

lay a finger on

to bother someone
Example: I was told not to lay a finger on my cousin
when we got to their house .

lend a hand

to help someone
Example: I went over to see if I could lend a hand .

live hand to mouth

to live day to day on little money
Example: since I only have a temporary job , I have
to live hand to mouth

not to lift a finger

not to do anything
Example: he never lifts a finger

old hand at something
a seasoned expert at something
Example: I'm an old hand at fixing cars

on hand
readily available
Example: Do you have a screwdriver on hand?

on ones heels
following closely behind somebody
Example: he fled from the stadium with the police on his heels

out of hand
out of control
Example: things really got out of hand when the police arrived

palm off
hard sell , sell or give by trickery
Example: whenever she goes for shopping , she got palmed off by salesclerk

press the flesh
shake hands
Example: they both pressed the flesh

put ones finger on something
to discover the truth
Example: I think you just put your finger on it

put ones foot in ones mouth
to say something that is the wrong thing to say in a situation
Example: I put my foot in my mouth and said that I didn't like fish just before my friends served fish at their dinner party .

put someone finger on
to decide , to determine
Example I can't put my finger on now

not to raise a hand
not to do something
Example: My mother says I don't raise a hand to her anytime .

right hand man
valuable partner
Example: he is my right hand man in college

rub elbows with someone
to socialize with someone
Example: when i went to Boston , i rubbed elbows with all the guys in college

second hand
used
Example: I bought my car second hand

short handed
low on personnel
Example: we were short handed at work today

somebody doesn't lift a finger
somebody doesn't do anything
Example: he doesn't even lift a finger

stick like a sore thumb
conspicuous , clear
Example: It sticks like a sore thumb ! why can't you get it?!

stickem up!
put your hand up , hands up!
Example: stickem up! Nobody moves!

have sticky fingers
the habit of stealing something
Example: everyone thinks that the new staff at work has sticky fingers as many things have been stolen recently

the right hand doesn't know what the left is doing
to be unaware of the actions of an associate
Example: one of the vice presidents of the company told me to buy the stock and the other told me not to ! obviously , the right hand doesn't know what the left is doing

throw up ones hands
admit that one can not succeed
Example: I threw up my hands in math exam when I understood that I cant solve it

try one's hand at something
to test one's ability at something
Example: tomorrow I'm going to try my hand at golf
.

twiddle ones thumb
to do nothing
Example: All the salesclerk in this passage just twiddle their thumb

under ones thumb
obedient to someone , controlled by someone
Example: I have her under my thumb now .

work ones fingers to the bone
to work very hard
Example: I have to work my fingers to the bone to live hand to mouth .

wrapped around one's little finger
to controlled by someone
Example: In a second you'll be wrapped around my little finger

Head

airhead
a silly, stupid person
Example: you are airhead with this airhead idea

big head
to be conceited
Example his head has gotten big over since he became a movie star

bite one's head off
to attack someone verbally
Example: I criticized her dress and she bite my head off

bonehead
a stupid person
Example: he is a real bonehead

Buddha Head
Someone of Asian descent
Example : Tim is a Buddha head

cakehead
Someone who is not very bright.
Example: That cakehead just ran that red light

chip-head
One who is obsessed with computers.
Example: He's such a chip-head he could draw you a
diagram of the internal cicuit of the Pentium 4
microprocessor

cool head
nice guy
Example: I was given help by cool head in subway to
find my path

cotton head
An elderly person.
Example: Traffic is very heavy this morning. There
are a lot of cotton heads on the road.

cranium crusher
to give someone a swift kick in the head
Example: man if Justin keeps this up I'm gonna give
him a cranium crusher he will never forget

crap head
One who forgets
Example: You were late picking me up, you crap head

dome
your head, above the face.
Example: John just got mugged! They slapped a lead pipe against his dome!

egg head
a good intelligent guy
Example : Mike is a egg head . he always knows what to do

go soak your head
to get lost
Example : just go soak your head!

have swelled head
to be conceited
Example: I don't like being around her . she has such a swelled head

head out
to depart
Example: let 's head out around 8:00 in the morning

head over heels for someone
madly in love with someone
Example: I'm head over heels for my teacher

heads are going to roll
people are going to get in trouble
Example: the boss just called them into his office . I think heads are gonna roll

headstrong
stubborn
Example: he is always so headstrong

hit the hail on the head
to be exactly right
Example you hit the nail on the head

hole in the head
to be crazy
Example: I think you've got a hole in your head

hothead
a quick tempered person
Example: he is such a hothead in every matter

make headway
to make progress
Example: you are starting to make headway with your French !

meathead
stupid person
Example: you are so meathead!

noggin
a person's head
Example: what's going on in your noggin?

off the top of one's head
a coarse estimate , without calculation
Example: I can 't be specific , but off the top of my head , I'd say he 'll be arriving in about five minutes

out of ones head
stupid
Example: he is out of his head

sorehead
grumbler or complainer .
Example: don't be such a sorehead

stick ones head in the sand
to pretend not to see the facts
Example: he didn't stick his head in the sand

swelled head
snobbish person
Example: I don' t like being around her . she has such
a swelled head!

talking head
a TV announcer in show when they talk and their
head is shown simply
Example: I'm so sick of talking heads

to be on a head trip
to be living in an imaginary world , dreaming
Example: she 's on a real head trip . she thinks she 's
the smartest person in class

use one's head
to use one's intelligence
Example : everything he does is stupid . he never
uses his head

Health

a dead loss
freeloader person
Example: he 's been staying in here for a long times and never ever pay anything . what a dead loss he is!

A ok
feel ok
Example: I really feel A ok now

eat
exhausted , ill
Example: I was so eat so I couldn't go to work

bite the dust
to die or be killed
Example: the old man finally bite the dust one day

buy it
 to die
Example: buy it stupid asshole!

buy the farm
to die
Example: he's too young to buy the farm

Carked it
Kicked the bucket.
Example: It hurt so bad I thought I had carked it

caught dead
never
Example: I wouldn't be caught dead in that case

check out
 to die
Example: I think he 's going to check out tonight

circling the drain
Preparing to die.
Example: That guy on life support is circling the drain

co-ollybobbles
Stomachache.
Example: If you eat those green apples, you'll get co-ollybobbles

croack
to die
Example: she croacked due to poverty

crook
being sick or unwell
Example: I can't come in to work today , I feel a bit crook

crump
to die on the way to the hospital
Example: The driver is hurt pretty bad, he'll probably crump on the way

dead
quiet, dull
Example: that was dead in all city today

dead duck
to get in trouble
Example: I was in dead duck and couldn't escape

dead easy
easy to do something
Example: repairing the computers is dead easy for me

dead serious
really serious
Example: I'm dead serious man , why don't u believe me?

deadbeat
a dull, lazy, unreliable person
Example: I don't like him . he 's so deadbeat

deadbeat dad
a father who doesn't pay child support regularly
Example: John was a deadbeat dad . he never helps to his sons to pay their rent

drop a body
To murder someone.
Example: If his crew keeps coming around, I may have to drop a body

dutch act
to kill him/her self
Example: she took the dutch act last night

eat it
to crash, wipe out, die.
Example: My car skidded off the road and ate it in a ditch. It's been a bad day

fagoogled
absolutely exhausted
Example: Bob was mountain biking in the bush, and after the last hill climb he was fagoogled.

fed up
depressed
Example: you look a bit fed up

get somebody
to kill somebody
Example: so if you don't tell me , I'm gonna get you

go under the knife
to have surgery
Example: she went under the knife yesterday

goner
near to go to die
Example: he thought his father is a goner

kick the bucket
to die
Example: finally he kicked the bucket in his house

knock off
to kill someone, to murder someone
Example: he was knocked off by a bunch of criminals

maxed out
exhausted
Example: I can't come out with you tonight . I'm a kind a maxed out

off
to murder, to kill
Example: yesterday some criminals attacked the little
girl and after rubbing her cell phone they off her .

out of it
not aware of what happening
Example: the woman was old but not really out of it

pass out
to die
Example: she thought he may even pass out

shatterd
be extremely upset
Example: I'm afraid , but he will be shattered if he
got the news

the big C
cancer
Example: Do you know how dangerous the big C is?

wiped out
exhausted
Example: I'm really wiped out , I can't hang out now

Heart

after one's own heart
well-kind for agreeing with one's own feeling ,
interest and ideas
Example : they are after their own heart .

at heart
in spite of , in reality
Example: I was a worker in the past at heart . but nowadays I'm working in the bank.

break one's heart
make very sad or hopeless
Example: after watching Leon movie , It broke my heart .

change of heart
a change in the way one feels about something
Example: by reading that romantic book , It changed of my heart .

cross one's heart and hope to die
to say that what one has said is surely true
Example: I didn't cross my heart and hope to die in my last interview .

eat one's heart out
want something , grieve long and hopelessly for something
Example: eat you heart out! I saw Beyonce in the street yesterday .

eat ones heart out
to be envious
Example: she is going to eat her heart out when she sees me with Tom

from the bottom of one's heart
with great feeling
Example: I felt sorry for her from the bottom of my heart .

from the heart
sincerely , honestly
Example: she said all the story from the heart .

get to heart of something
to get the core of something
Example: we should get to heart of it and inform everybody

have heart
be encouraged , feel braver and want to try
Example: you don't have heart to talk to her!?

have one's heart set on
want something very much
Example: when I was a kid , I had my heart set on my computer .

heart goes out
one feels sorry for
Example: her heart goes out to Jason .

heart is in the right place
kindhearted
Example: my mother is a kind person . her heart is in the right place .

heart of gold
a kind , generous nature
Example: she has a heart of gold .

heart of stone
a nature without pity
Example: is the death penalty heart of stone and unusual punishment .

heart skips a beat
to be settled or excited from surprise
Example: she can't wait for her party . her heart skips a beat

heart to heart
a serious discussion
Example I need to have a heart to heart with my son .

heartache
anguish
Example every time he came home late , he caused me heartache

heavy heart
a feeling of being weighed down with sorrow , unhappiness
Example: he miss his son in accident . he has a heavy heart now .

lose heart
to be disappointed
Example: don't lose your heart! Just rely on God .

open one's heart
to talk about one's feeling honestly , to talk over to someone
Example: don't open your heart in front of him .

wear one's heart on one's sleeve
to talk over someone
Example: she came to me and wore her heart on my sleeve

with all one's heart
with great feeling , sincerely
Example: I like to say I love you mom with all my heart .

Heels

Achilles' heel
vulnerable area
Example: If you want her to like you , just talk about animals . that's her Achilles' heel

be a heel
contemptible person
Example: I feel like a heel . I wanted to give him a hand

cool one's heels
to wait
Example: I cooled my heels for a whole hour before she finally arrived

drag one heels
to delay
Example: quite dragging your heels and hurry !

head over heels for someone
madly in love with someone
Example: we are head over heels for my sister's husband

heel
contemptible person
Example: Jack is such a heel person .

kick up one's heel
frolic
Example: I can't wait to go on vacation . I need to kick up my heels

walk on one's heels
to walk too closely to someone
Example: stop walking on my heels!

Insult

a case of the ass or redass
highly annoyed, pissed off.
Example: Sergeant Greenfield has this huge case of the ass with me ever since I wrecked his jeep.

absogoddamnlutelyz
Ultimate absolutely.
Example: I am absogodamnlutely sure I've locked the door

ace
ass, fool
Example: I ran into a wall today, and felt like an ace.

air ahead
stupid guy
Example: you think he can give you a hand?! he 's a airhead as I know

Amish ass-crack of dawn
Early morning hours, before 9 am.
Example: Why do I have a 9 o'clock class? I have to get up at the Amish ass-crack of dawn

arse-licking
saying nice things to someone in order to get something from them
Example: finally , he got his mark from master by arse licking

as bare as your ass
conspicuous , noticeable , obvious
Example: that question is as bare as your ass . why don't you get it!

ass-kisser
someone who says nice things to someone in order to get something from them
Example: Mike is a ass kisser

Assariffic
Something that is not good.
Example: My weekend was assariffic! Friday I got pulled over and Sunday I lost my homework.

assness
Smartass , wise guy
Example: Thanks a lot, assness!

ate up with the dumb ass
When someone is really dull or stupid.
Example: Look at that guy. He's really ate up with the dumb ass

back number
stupid
Example: shut up back number!

badass
A tough guy.
Example: he 's so badass . you cant convince him

bag your face
go away , get lost
Example: I hate you , bag your face!

bahoozle
Jerk, fool, moron-- an irritating person
Example: That bahoozle just took my parking space.

bastard
an unpleasant, despicable person
Example: come over here bastard

batty
crazy
Example: he 's a real batty

bean brain
to be stupid
Example: that girl is so bean brain

beat it
go away , get lost
Example: you are getting on my nerve , beat it!

belch
to burp
Example: He always belch at the food table

berk
stupid
Example: stop doing that berk!

blimp
fat person
Example: look at that blimp who just came in

bonehead
a stupid person
Example: he 's a real bonehead

bonkers
crazy
Example: you 're bonkers to rent the place without seeing it first

boob
stupid
Example: Hey boob , what do you want?

bug off
get lost , go away
Example: I hate you . bug off!

bugger off
to go away
Example: I don't wanna see you face anymore . bugger off!

candy ass
timid guy
Example: that candy ass make me sick

chent
a complete dimwit
Example: that guy is a total chent

Chicamawaka
A person that is acting like an idiot
Example: Some of my friends are such chicamawakas

chicken shit
coward person
Example: he 's such a chicken shit

collywally
Someone who is crazy
Example: Eddie just jumped off a building. He's a collywally

crunk
crazy
Example: man , he 's crunk!

cuckoldafied
To be made a cuckold.
Example: Was I cuckoldafied when he kissed my girlfriend?

daffy
idiot
Example: she is acting daffy , because she is so happy

DaQ
To be a complete idiot.
Example: How did you fail that easy test, you DaQ?

dench
A person who acts like a idiot , acts stupidly .
Example: Stop acting like a dench.

dilbry
idiot, foolish.
Example: You broke it! well, your 're a dilbry aren't you

dildo
stupid
Example: you act like a dildo .

dipshit
stupid
Example: she 's dipshit

dipstick
Idiot, moron, stupid person.
Example: He knew the ice on the lake was only an inch thick. But the dipstick walked on it and fell through, anyway!

dobber
Someone who is acting dumb, stupid, silly.
Example: Quit being such a dobber.

dobo
A name for someone who does something idiotic.
Example: Great move, dobo.

dooley
A person who tries to look or act cool but really comes off like a moron.
Example: Check out Dooley over there acting like a moron.

dope
stupid
Example: you are such a dope

Drongo
dense or stupid person
Example: You drongo!

dumb bunny
stupid person
Example: what a dumb bunny !

dumb dora
stupid
Example: come here dumb dora .

dumbass
idiot
Example: what's your name dumbass?

dummy
stupid
Example: Your aunt can be such a dummy
sometimes

dweeb
a studious but socially inept person
Example: she is such a dweeb

fag
stupid
Example: what you doing fag?

fart around
to screw around , to waste time , dally
Example: I wish you 'd stop farting around and help
me clean up

fatso
a fat person
Example: he go married with a fatso girl

flap ones gums
to talk nonsense
Example: Stop flapping your gums !

Flatliner
a very stupid, or very disorganized person
Example: YO! 'Flatliner',The RED light means
STOP!

flip a bitch
Make a u-turn.
Example: I missed my street. Gonna have to flip a
bitch at the next light

Fool brain
Someone not real bright, an idiot.
Example: Frank often slams his fingers in the car
door. What a fool brain he is

freeloader
freeloader
Example: He came to my house and stayed for 2
weeks , what a freeloader he is!

fresh
rude person
Example: My friend is a really fresh guy

get out of my face
get lost
Example: get out of my face little sucker!

get the hell out of here
get lost
Example: get the hell out of here before I call the cops

give a shit to sth
not to care about something or someone
Example: I don't give a shit to him

give it a rest
shut up
Example: you are talking nonsense. give it a rest

go chase yourself
get lost
Example: go chase yourself now and never ever come again!

go climb a tree
get lost
Example: he told me go climb a tree

go fry an egg
get lost
Example: go fry an egg

go jump in the lake
get lost
Example: go jump in the lake

hare-brained
stupid, foolish
Example: the girl at party was hare brained . did you see her?

have you flipped?
have you gone crazy?
Example: She is not gonna call you , have you flipped?

hick
stupid
Example: he 's a hick guy . don't talk to him

horse shit
nonsense
Example: all his talking is just a horse shit

horse's ass
fool
Example: he's such a horse's ass

horsefeathers
nonsense
Example: stop saying horsefeathers

hot air
nonsense
Example: all that was hot air he said

idiot-box
TV
Example: turn on that damn idiot box

jack shit
nothing , very little
Example: I just can lend you jack shit bucks now

jackass
fool
Example: Don't be such a jackass!

jerk
stupid
Example: she 's so jerk as I know!

knucklehead
stupid
Example: our boss was a knucklehead

kook
a strange or eccentric person
Example: you can' get what he 's doing , he ' s kook person

lardass
fat guy
Example: she 's lost 25 pound . but still she 's lardass

loco
crazy, insane
Example: there 's a lot of loco around here . be careful

loony
a silly person
Example: your new girlfriend is a real loony

loony bin
a hospital for mentally ill people
Example: he 's loony . but he doesn't go to loony bin to be treated

loopy
eccentric, a little crazy
Example: you are loopy if you think I'm gonna marry her

loser
person without any good qualities
Example: you can see losers here with you own eyes!

louse
an unpleasant or nasty person
Example: my friend is a louse . he takes a shower
once blue in the moon

mister wonderful
horrible person
Example: he 's a mister wonderful

no no
something must not say or do
Example: when I was young , public kissing was a no
no

noise
nonsense , bullshit
Example: what a bunch of noise!

noodle head
stupid person
Example: what a noodle head he is!

old hat
stupid
Example: look at old hat over there . he 's Jason

one's can't tell shit from shinola
when somebody doesn't know the difference between
two things
Example: you can't tell shit from shinola

out to lunch
crazy
Example: he 's out to lunch

pea brain
stupid person
Example: he is such a pea brain

Piss off
Go away!
Example: piss off man loser!

prat
fool , stupid
Example: that's your prat girl?

schmuck
stupid
Example: you 're a schmuck if you wanna buy that
car

screwy idea
crazy idea
Example: what the screwy idea , said the other man

scumbag
a worthless or very disliked person
Example: she never knows how to treat a boy . she 's
a scumbag

shit head
stupid
Example: are you shit head or what?!

smeghead
stupid
Example: what's your job smeghead?

stuffed shirt
someone who shows off a lot about him/herself
Example: she 's stuffed shirt in this class

swear up a blue streak
to swear and curse excessively
Example: she can really swear up a blue streak!

tool
a stupid person
Example: the man working in pub is a tool

tub of lard
very fat
Example: you are so tub of lard . you need to lose some damn weight

twirp
a silly, immature person
Example: he can't pass the driving test at first . he 's twirp

yahoo
a rude and aggressive person
Example: he is a real yahoo to me

yokel
A dumb person who never seems to get anything right.
Example: James is a yokel when it comes to math

you all got the same rap!
Same situation
Example: you all got the same rap!

You are the weakest link.... Go
get lost
Example: You are the weakest link.... Go.

you have got a screw loose
you are crazy!
Example: you've got a screw loose again!

yutnut
an fool, an imbecile
Example: Those yutnuts in marketing always forget their passwords!

Leave

audi
To leave.
Example: I'm audi.

Audi Like Five Geez
To leave quickly.
Example: I'm Audi Like Five Geez, gee

boogy
to leave very fast
Example: when we can boogy?

book
to leave very fast
Example: I'm gonna book

cheese it
to leave quickly,
Example: Let's cheese it, then

cut out
to leave
Example: I will cut it out tomorrow

delete yourself
To go away or leave.
Example: Melissa, you are really starting to annoy me. Would you please just delete yourself?

Dine 'n' Dash
eat and leave without paying. eat and run.
Example: The food and service at the restaurant was so bad the group decided to dine and dash

dip
to leave somewhere quickly
Example: I'm about to dip to the store and get gallon of milk

Ditch
finish, stop doing,
Example: This sucks, let's ditch.

get out of someone face
to leave someone alone
Example: get out of my face , I'm busy now

history
to leave
Example: It's 11:00 , I'm history

jam
to leave the area
Example: he ' s jamming . don't you like to see her again?

jump
to leave without permission, to move illegally
Example: I jumped from school when I understood we got a exam

make tracks
to leave somewhere
Example: I'm tracking tracks , don't you wanna come?

take a hike
leave
Example: you gotta take a hike otherwise they will get you out

take off
to leave
Example: we ' d better take off now if we don't want to be late

vamoose
to depart quickly
Example: give me a low down when you wanna vamoose?

Like

all about
Used to show intense enthusiasm.
Example: Guys, I'm all about leaving. Yeah, well, I'm all about finishing my burger.

bag
interest , taste
Example: sailing has never really was a bag for me

do you fancy
would you like
Example: do you fancy to go to party?

fancy
like
Example: I rather fancy the new car

get a kick out of
to enjoy something really
Example: I get a kick out of watching horror movie

get the hot for someone
like somebody
Example: I think she's got the hot for him

Love

Adorable
Really adorable and cute.
Example: Look at that guy, he's adorable!

ambiamorous
Loving two people at the same time.
Example: I can't choose between Harvey or Stanley. I'm totally ambiamourous.

crush
a strong feeling of love or infatuation for someone
Example: I have a deep crush on her

Enamorable
Able to be loved in a very cute way.
Example: Am I not enamorable? purrr

fall for a girl
to go falling love with a girl
Example: he falls for a girl in his college

floydian
One who loves the band Pink Floyd. (Also used in floydian slip.)
Example: Bob saw Pink Floyd in concert 12 times. He's a floydian

have a heart
to have compassion
Example: he has a heat to me

have heart go out to someone
to feel compassion for someone
Example: my heart goes out to her

make fish eyes at someone
to look at someone in a lovely way
Example: he 's making fish eyes at me

Medical

at death's door
very near to death , to be goner
Example: he is at death's door .

back on one's feel
physical healthy again
Example: he is back on his feel again .

black out
to lose consciousness , to faint
Example: as soon as she saw the body , she was
blacked out

break out
being showing a rash or other skin disorder
Example: I'm breaking out again , I should see
doctor

breath one's last
to die , bite the dust
Example: finally after standing so much pain , he
breathed his last yesterday .

bring around
to restore health
Example: will you be able to bring around him ,
Doctor?

catch one's death of cold
to become very ill
Example: he catch his death of cold and has stayed in
home about 2 weeks .

check up
a periodic inspection of a patient by a doctor
Example: Doctor told me to have check up after that accident .

clean bill of health
a reporter certificate that a person is healthy
Example: I don't have clean bill of health . I have to get it as soon as possible .

come down
to become sick
Example: she came down and couldn't come to office today .

draw blood
to make someone blood , get blood from someone
Example: I don't like to draw blood .

fall ill
to become sick
Example: after playing soccer under the rain , he fell ill .

flare up
to begin again suddenly illness
Example: my headache starts to flare up . I need to visit Doctor .

go under the knife
to be operated on in surgery
Example: last year John had an bad accident . but he didn't go under the knife .

head shrinker
a phychiatrist
Example: is there any head shrinker around here ?

just what the doctor ordered
exactly what is needed or wanted
Example: just what the doctor ordered take your pill on time .

look the picture of health
to become better , on the mend
Example: your looking the picture of health . It's good for you

out cold
in a faint
Example: he felt out cold from hunger .

over the worst
recovering from the illness
Example: be man! Just over the worst! You can do it!

pull through
to recover from serious illness
Example: he seems ok now . I think he's pulling through after 2 month .

run a temperature
to have a higher than normal body temperature
Example: I'm running a temperature . I hope it's not the flu .

run some test
when a doctor does some medical tests on a patient
Example: will you run some test on him doctor?

take a turn for the worse
to become sicker
Example: she took a turn for the worse .

under ther weather
not feeling well
Example: what's up man? Under the weather .

Mistakes

a'stake
a mistake
Example: I'm sorry, I made a'stake

all wet
completely wrong
Example: the answer was all wet .

blew something big time
to make a big mistake
Example: this time , he blew it big time

screw up
to make a serious mistake
Example: he screwed up and wore his father's shirt

you got me twisted
You've mistaken me for someone else or It wasn't me. A response to a teacher or classmate when they blame something on you and you know you didn't do it.
Example: Teacher: Why did you do that? Student: You got me twisted

Money

a buck three eighty
The price for anything.
Example: how much is this, sir? That's a buck three eighty

a-dollar-three-eighty
The price for anything.
Example: How much is it? A-dollar-three-eighty.

a dollar three eighty five
A nonsensical price for when one does not want to give the real price.
Example: How much did your Lexus cost? A dollar three eighty five

a double
A twenty dollar bill.
Example: I've got eighty dollars on me, all I need is a double to make it a hundred

a fin
Five dollars
Example: All I have is a fin and two dollars in change in my pocket

a nifty
A fifty dollar bill.
Example: I borrowed a nifty from my mom and she upped it five bucks more. Now I owe her fifty-five dollars

a sleeve
A hundred dollar bill.
Example: I got seven hundred dollars, all in sleeves.

bad paper
untrusted cheque
Example: she got in jail because of his bad papers

baking donuts
To go out and make money. Going to work. Earn your living with a job
Example: What you doing tonight? Baking donuts.

bottom dollar
all of money
Example: how much bucks you have? i have 10$ bottom dollar

bread
money
Example: how much bread have u got?

broke
have no money
Example: I'm broke , don't ask me any buck

buck
dollar , money
Example: how much buck do you need?

c
1000$
Example: how much C's do you need ?

cabbage
money
Example: how much cabbage do i owe you?

cake
lots of money
Example: That Bill Gates is rolling in cake!

cash money millionaire
Someone who has a lot of money
Example: My uncle is a cash money millionaire

cashola
money
Example: I will come for a drink but I've got to get some cashola first

cheddar
money, cash.
Example: That guy must have mad cheddar to be driving that Benz

chicken feed
make very little money
Example: I made a chicken feed last year

clam
dollar
Example: he stole sixty clams from me!

clock dollars
To earn money.
Example: My new job allows me to clock dollars

cut a check
write a check
Example: we will cut the check tonight

dead presidents
money
Example: The bank holds a lot of dead presidents.

dosh
dollar
Example: I'm taking you out tonight, as I'm flush
with dosh

double sawbuck
twenty dollar bill.
Example: Zack owes me a double saw buck

dough
money
Example: how much dough you need?

dough-nut
One crazy about money.
Example: You'll never satisfy her, she's a dough-nut.

Dove
name for a $10 dollar bill
Example: Yo, can I borrow 2 doves ?

downtown foldies
money
Example: you want to go to the bar tonight? I can't. I don't have any downtown foldies

ducketts
money
Example: Can you hook me up with some ducketts till I get paid

earn one's keep
to earn own money
Example: I earn my keep by translating texts in college

earner
a good source of money
Example: my earner is my daddy

easy money
money that get without effort
Example: he is looking for easy money

el cheapo
very cheap
Example: that car is really el cheapo

Ends
money
Example: these days without ends you cant survive

face card
a one hundred dollar bill.
Example: Sam passed Will a face card

fat grip of scrilla
To have on hand a large sum of cash.
Example: I just got paid, and I'm about to have a fat grip of scrilla

Fiddy
fifty dollars.
Example: When are you going to pay me back that fiddy?

finsky
$5 bill
Example: Loan me a finsky.

fiver
five dollar or pound
Example: I only have a fiver, so I can't pay for dinner

foot the bill
to pay the bill
Example: I didn't have to pay the bill. she said he would foot the entire bill

fron money
money that should pay for renting a place
Example: you have not paid your fron money yet

grand
thousand $
Example: how much dollar is this cell phone? grand

green back
money
Example: he makes a lot of money as a contractor

Gs

thousand $

Example: Don't worry , tell me how much Gs you need?

hand out

the money that pays in charity

Example: whenever we go on a trip , my mother pays hand out

its on me

means , I pay the money

Example: don't worry pal . It's on me

jack

money

Example: the job wasn't exciting , but the jack was good

lettuce

money

Example: without lettuce you cant survive

make killing

make a lot of money

Example : I made a killing in casino last day

mega bucks

lots of money

Example: I think I don't need any mega bucks anymore

moola

money

Example: tell me how much moola you need to invest on it?

nest egg
lots of money that you save over the years
Example: you need to have nest egg to go to abroad

on me
at my expense
Example: this time it is not on me dude . you gotta
pay for it

peanuts
very little money
Example: all I have is a peanuts . you know?

quarter
a U.S. or Canadian 25-cent coin
Example: Do you have quarter ?

quid
money (pounds)
Example: do you know how much quid they need?

rolling in it
really rich guy
Example : I'm rolling in it , I will pay , don't worry

yuppie food stamp
twenty dollar bill
Example: Let me go to the ATM and get a few
yuppie food stamps

Mouth

bad mouth
a person who says curse all the time
Example: he 's so bad mouth , don't talk to him anymore

big mouth
talkative
Example: being such a big mouth is a real problem

blabbermouth
a talker
Example: don't tell her any secrets . he is a real blabbermouth

dirty mouth
face card
Example: my friend is dirty mouth

down in the mouth
depressed
Example: you look down in the mouth . what 's wrong?

edge
this is a synonym for 'mouth'
Example: shut your edge!

fat lip
a swollen lip from getting punched in the mouth
Example: stop teasing me or I'll give you a fat lip

garbage mouth
face card person
Example: I don't like to hang out with John , he's a garbage mouth .

kisser
mouth
Example: Doctor told me to open my kisser .

loud mouth
talkative
Example: Jane is a loud mouth person as I know .

mouth
language
Example how many mouth do u know?

mouth off
to speak rudely
Example Jack became angry and started to mouth off

run off at the mouth
to talk nonstop
Example: stop running off at the mouth

shoot off one's mouth
to say whatever comes to one's mind
Example: think a little before you go shooting off your mouth

Name

adda be
Congratulatory phrase, often used in a sarcastic manner.
Example: Your girlfriend just slapped you in front of the whole school? Adda be doofus

Alice
A generic name given to someone who is bothering you. Not limited to females.
Example: Hey, Alice, if you can't drive it, park it.

Amiland
German nickname for the USA.
Example: Next summer holidays, I'll go to Amiland.

angus
To become very angry and possibly hurt someone
Example: So what happened then? I just started to get all angus and had to leave before I slapped him upside the head

big bertha
a fat woman
Example: his mom is a big bertha

big john
police
Example : watch out big john is coming

by George!
use for surprise
Example: by George ! you passed the exam!

charley horse
a painful muscle cramp in one's leg
Example: why are you limping? I've got a charley horse in my leg

Choke N' Puke
Canadian's nickname for McDonalds.
Example: Where do you want to eat tonight? Let's go to Choke N' Puke

Colin
related to intestines
Example: I've got a pain in my Colin

Da Burgh
slang for Pittsburgh, Pennsylavania
Example: Wanna go down to Da Burgh to watch the Penguins?

Devil-Billy
A proper noun used to describe someone who is acting in an outrageous or devious manner.
Example: You replaced the vanilla ice cream with lard? You're the Devil-Billy

don juan
a handsome boy
Example: Oh look at her new boyfriend . he is such a don juan

doubting thomas
a very doubtful person
Example: I don't mean to be a doubting thomas , but I don't believe him

earl
vomit
Example: you know the meaning of earl?

Eliot Ness
a perfect girl
Example: Don't even step, she's an Eliot Ness

Eugene
nerd or geek.a person that is not cool.unpopular
Example: what a Eugene. yuk! He's a eugene.I would
never date him, he's a big Eugene

Flippin' Nora
 To be completely shocked about something. An
exclamation of complete shock from up north.
Example: 'Flippin' Nora! I can't believe she did that.

 for pete's sake
a word of surprise
Example: I'm afraid that all the time we have , for
pet's sake

for the love of pete !
for surprise
Example: for the love of pete ! how could she paint
something so awful ?

fritz out
to cease to operate
Example: my radio just fritzed out

Geez , Louise!
for surprise
Example: geez , louise ! why did you spend all your money on that?

guy
man in general
Example: do you know that guy?

have something down pat
know everything about something
Example: I have slang down pat

heaven's to betsy
exclamation for surprise
Example: heaven's to betsy ! look who's there ! It's so good to see you again

hit the road , jack!
leave!
Example: let's hit the road , jack

holy joe
a religious guy in church
Example: my daddy is a holy joe

jack
anything
Example: he doesn't know jack about computer

jack around
waste around
Example: stop jack around . come and give me a hand

jack-of-all-trades
a person who does everything
Example: my dad is jack of all trades , he can fix everything

jack shit
nothing
Example: he doesn't know jack shit about computer game

jack someone around
to mislead someone
Example: car salesman always jack you around

Jackie
quickly
Example: I will go to home and come back jackie

Jackshit
nothing , zilch
Example: there is jackshit to be worried about anymore

Jeeze Louise
a word of surprise
Example: Jeeze Louise! You won the lottery?!

Joe
coffee
Example: a cup of Joe please

Joe blow
man in general , guy
Example: who's that Joe blow?

Joe schmoe
man in general , guy , man
Example : all Joe schmoe are equal in the sight of the law

John
bathroom , restroom
Example: where is the nearesrt John around here?

John hancock
signature
Example: could you give me a John hancock

John Q. public
an ordinary person
Example: that guy over there is a John Q.public

Johnny on the spot
very quickly , immediately
Example: he arrived Johnny on the spot

Josh
to tease someone, usually in a friendly way
Example: he was joshed in front of his girlfriend in his office

Jow blow
everyone
Example: Jow blow is quiet! I need to study now

know someone from Adam
to be completely unfamiliar with someone
Example: I don't know him from Adam

46. Mary Jane
marijuana
Example: they were arrested due to Mary Jane

no way , Jose!
absolutely not
Example: would you pass me the cake ? no way, Jose!

on the fritz
inoperable
Example: the TV is on the fritz

peeping tom
a spy person
Example: a man who spies in windows: there 's a peeping tom outside my window!

peter out
to diminish and decrease in energy
Example: I was strong in the beginning of the race but petered out near the end

plain jane
plain person
Example: he is so plain Jane

quicker than you can say jackie robinson
very quickly
Example: I'll be back quicker than you can say jackie robinson

ralph
to vomit
Example: I'm so full , I could ralph

rob Peter to pay Paul
Example: she's actually going to sell all of her furniture in order to have enough money to go on her trip . talk about robbing Peter to pay Paul !

Roger!
communication received
Example: you gotta go to middle of them and kill that skinny guy . roger!

scrooge
a miser , stingy person
Example: don't bother him to donate to the charity , he's such a scrooge

Tom , Dick and Harry
each and every man
Example: you expect me to give money to every tom Dick and Harry who approaches me?

tomfoolery
foolishness
Example: stop this tomfoolery at once!

uncle Sam
the united state government , tax man
Example: uncle Sam takes money out of my paycheck each week

willy-nilly
haphazardly
Example: since he was in a hurry , he chose which shirt to wear willy-nilly

Yes siree , Bob
absolutely
Example: will u come to party with us? yes siree , Bob!

Nose

amersham
The sneeze that doesn't quite come.
Example: AAAAaaaaaaa... That was one hell of an amersham

as plain as the nose on one's face
very obvious , conspicuous
Example: It 's as plain as the nose on your face . why cant you get it !

brown noser
sycophant
Example: I hate brown nosers

chlomostlestangerine
klom-os-tl-stan-ger-een. The way your nose feels when it's stuffy and really dry inside. You can do nothing about it.
Example: do you feel that smell ? no , I'm chlomostlestangerine

cuggin
Chunk of hard snot found in your nose.
Example: Look at that cuggin in Trevor's nose

cut off ones nose to spite ones face
to make things worse for oneself because one is very angry at someone else
Example: he was working on computer . suddenly , cut off his nose to spite his face

get one's nose out of joint
to become offended
Example: don't get your nose out of joint man .

hard nosed
stubborn
Example: you are always so hard nosed

have a nose for something
to have a knack for finding something
Example: she has a nose for finding bargains

have one's nose in the air
to be snobbish
Example: she never talks to me . she always has her nose in the air

have ones nose in something
unwelcome interest in something , impolite curiosity
Example: he has his nose in everything .

honker
big nose
Example don't you remember that honker she used to have?

It's no skin off my nose
its non of my business
Example: whether she comes to my party or not , it's no skin off my nose

keep one's nose to the grindstone
to work hard
Example: If you keep your nose to the grindstone
you will succeed

look down ones nose
think of as worthless
Example: she looked down me nose

nose dive
to fail suddenly
Example: his health took a nose dive

nose- job
a surgery in somebody's nose
Example: how much does a nose-job cost?

nose out
to slightly defeat
Example: he nosed him out of the competition .

nosey
curious
Example: my friend is a nosey guy

pay through the nose
to pay a lot of money
Example: I had to pay through the nose to get that
dress

poke one's nose in someone's business
to meddle in someone's business
Example: he came over to poke his nose in my
business

pull the wool over ones nose
to deceive someone
Example: he pulled the wool over my nose and sold this car to me

right under one's nose
to be obvious
Example: the answer is right under your nose

take a nose dive
to fail suddenly
Example: his health took a nose dive

turn one's nose up at someone or something
to refuse and neglect someone
Example: she turned up her nose at the dinner

Number

algebras
Phone number
Example: That honey's cute . give her my algebras

behind the eight ball
in a difficult position
Example: oh man , again we are behind the eight ball

catch-23
in order to solve a problem one has to create a larger problem.
Example: Bill pulled a Catch-23 when he saved 20 people at the cost of killing

Centurysquared
The 10,000th.
Example: This is the centurysquared word to enter the dictionary

deep six someone
to kill someone
Example: I want you to go deep six him

deuce-and-a-quarter
Reflects the number 225.
Example: That will cost you a deuce-and-a-quarter.
Back in the day I drove a deuce-and-a-quarter

dressed to the nines
extremely fancily dressed
Example :what up man ! you dressed to the nine .

eighty-eight
piano
Example there is my old eighty-eight

eighty-six
to get rid of
Example: in order to eighty-six him , what should I do!

elevendy-three
To avoid giving a true number when questioned.
Example: How old are you mister? elevendy-three

eleventeen
Imaginary number which occurs right after nineteen and 'tenteen.'
Example: I've got eleventeen rabbits

eleventeener
girl that's too young.
Example: When your friend is checking out a girl and you notice that she's eleventeen

fat to the fifth
obese
Example: Why is it that many teachers nowadays are fat to the fifth?

fifty footer
person who looks attractive from a distance, but gets progressively more ugly with proximity
Example: I thought she was pretty . but she was fifty footer

five across the face
a slap across the face
Example: That boy better shut up before he gets the five across the face

Five by five
Everything's great, couldn't be better.
Example: Hey, how are you? Five by five.

five-finger discount
Shoplifting
Example: Q. Where'd you get that? A. It was a five-finger discount

fivehead
Balding male's big forehead.
Example: He doesn't have a forehead. He's got a fivehead

from day one
right from the start
Example: he was mean to me from day one

get the third degree
to be interrogated
Example: as soon as I got home , my mom got me the third degree

gimme five!
give me five fingers
Example: my friend told me , gimme five!

give someone five
to shake hand with somebody
Example :she didn't give me five

give someone the once over
to scrutinize someone
Example: you should have seen how his brothers and sisters gave me the once over when they met me for the first time

goody two shoes
an ostentatiously virtuous person
Example: she is such a goody two shoes

grab forty winks
to take a nap
Example: I'm going to grab forty winks before we leave

If I've told you once , I've told you a thousand times
means , I have told u so many time
Example: If I've told you once , I've told you a thousand times , he is lying !

in seventh heaven
in a good feeling , in a ecstasy
Example: I was in a seventh heaven when I got to LA

L7
stupid
Example: you won't believe it how L7 he is!

like two peas in a pod
identical
Example: those twins are like two peas in a pod

never in a million years
absolutely never
Example: I'll never learn how to swim in a million years

on cloud nine
euphoria
Example: ever since she met Tom , she 's been on cloud nine

one-in-a-million
exceptional
Example: you 're one in a million !

six o one , hal a dozen of the other
to amount to the same thing , to make no difference
Example: you can either meet us before the show for dinner or afterwards for dessert. It's six of one , half a dozen of the other

twenty-three skidoo
to leave
Example: I'm twenty-three skidoo

zero
a worthless person, someone who's done nothing worthwhile in life
Example: you 're dating him ? he 's such a zero !

Other

bash
party
Example: I was invited to big bash

beemer
B.M.W
Example: I 'll buy a new brand beemer today

blade
a knife
Example: we took plastic blades and forks on our picnic

blow
to waste something, such as money or an opportunity
Example: you 're blowing your money . be careful !

bunch
a lot
Example: what's bunch of money !

cage
slang for a car.
Example: Man, that cage almost hit me broadside.

canasta glasses
Eyeglasses with the long chain attached, like
librarians and old ladies wear.
Example: Al Davis looks so stupid wearing those
canasta glasses

case of the zactlies
exactly
Example: are you sure about it? case of the zactlies

cashed
Done, finished.
Example: Put your cigarette out, it's cashed.

catch
catch you later. Talk to you later, see you later....
Example: Catch

celly
a cell phone
Example: Just call me up on my celly

check
agree
Example: do you agree to come to party? check!

Cheech-marin
To wait or remain in one place for an additional period of time.
Example: Don't leave yet. Let's cheech-marin here for a while

chilling
Doing not much. Just hanging around.
Example: What did you do yesterday after school? Nothing much, just chilling

chip
fine, OK, all right
Example: Bert: Can I borrow your car, John ? chip !

chockablock
completely full of people or things, crammed full
Example: that's a chockablock club! Nobody could find each other!

chow down
eat a lot of food
Example: she chowed down in her party

clicklur
Remote control
Example: gimme the clicklur. This show's a rerun.

clunker
old car
Example: my girlfriend has got a clunker

cold a hellen
a very cold weather
Example: I won't go out of home in cold a hellen day

cop-out
to avoid
Example: if you want to lose weight , cop out eating between meals

crapsmack
Many, a lot
Example: Rachel has so crapsmack friends that I couldn't invite them all

creeled
to twist or sprain
Example: My brother fell and creeled his ankle.

Dadnasticate
To procrastinate, but feel kind a bad about doing it.
Example: If only I had started sooner. But, blast it, I've been dadnasticating all week.

darn tootin'
Agreeing with strongly.
Example: Do you want to go to the mall tonight? Darn tootin!

dashenka
slang for daring.
Example: You are just my little dashenka

data-dink
A computer expert.
Example: Call the data-dinks, the system has crashed again

derstand

To not comprehend, to be confused--opposite of understand.

Example: Sorry, I derstand you. Please repeat the question

destinkify

to shower, or, in noun form, the shower.

Example: hey yo! . Go destinkify.

diddly

nothing.

Example: It doesn't mean diddly to me.

diddly-squat

anything

Example: is there diddly squat I can do to help?

Dish

Date

Example: I've got a dish with a good looking guy

dispangular

anywhere

Example: I think this survey is totally dispangular.

do me a solid

used in reference to asking a favor

Example: Yo, do me a solid and pass me that eraser.

dodobber

a name for anything you don't know the name for.

Example: While putting together the computer desk, I couldn't figure out where the little oblong dodobber went

dohickey
known as the thingamajigger, whatchamacallit or that thing that you don't know the name of.
Example: Hey, Bob, what's that little dohickey do?

dolled up
Dressing up, embellishing.
Example: A: I sold the car as soon as I dolled it up a little

doobery-sprocket
something or someone you can't remember the name of
Example: Oh, look over there it's erm... doobery-sprocket

doognoobit
Interjection used to express anger, irritation, or disappointment.
Example: doognoobit! I forgot my pen in my locker!

downslaught
torrential rain
Example: I can't believe the Christmas lights stayed up with that downslaught we had last night

duck-turd
a cigar
Example: Hey Jeff, give me a puff of that duck-turd

dunno
do not know
Example: where is Sam? dunno

ecofreak
a person with strong views on the importance of
protecting the natural environment
Example: my ex girl friend was a ecofreak

everything is copa?
everything is setting pretty?
Example: what up man? everything is copa?

fab-flippin-tastic
Something that is incredibly good, so saying it's
fantastic isn't enough, you have to combine three
words to express your joy!
Example: That movie was fab-flippin-tastic!

fall off
to become less popular
Example : he fell off from all his fan

faloney
Full of baloney
Example: You must be kidding me. You are faloney.

fat chance
never
Example: do you want to go to that restaurant?

fen
to make a decision.
Example: I fen to meet her and talk to her

fiddadle
to go away and do something
Example: you're annoying me, go fiddadle

finna
another way of saying going to or gonna.
Example: I finna go to the store. Or, I ain't finna go to work today

fizz
cop
Example: Put that out, here comes a fizz! police

flick
movie
Example: what's your favorite flick jack?

Flicker Flacker
The remote control for the television
Example: Hey... where did you put the flicker flacker, my shows on! controle television

flinkelflank
remote control for TV
Example: I can't change the channel because I don't have the flinkelflank. Do you know where the flink is?

flipper
Remote contol, particularly for the television.
Example: This show's a rerun , gimme the flipper

flockynockynihiliphilipication
somethng that doesn' have a clear meaning , whatnot
Example: what's the name of that flockynockyniliphilipication? Oh It rings my bell now . that was John

Flog

to sell

Example: how much dollar you wanna flog it?

floochie

when with our mouth make a baby laugh

Example: when I was a child my parent got used to make a floochie on me

flooped

stumbled.

Example: The girl with all the dishes just flooped by me because she couldn't see and tripped over the chair

fo'sheazy

For sure

Example: Friend: You going to the party tonight. fo'sheazy

hang out

to spend time with friend outdoor

Example: do you want to come with me to hang out around the bar?

have a blast

have a great time

Example: we had a blast in your party

have someone on something

to be suited for somebody

Example: the thread that I wore , had my name on it

it will be a cold day in hell
never
Example: It will be a cold day in hell before I meet her

itty-bitty / itsy-bitsy
very small
Example: what an itsy-bitsy car!

kerfuffle
a noisy dispute, a commotion
Example: there was a kerfuffle outside the embassy

knock
to criticize someone or something
Example: It's a lot easier to knock than to offer useful suggestion

lingo
language, dialect
Example: He speaks six foreign lingo

pee
to urinate (v.) ,urine(n)
Example: daddy stop the car . I'm gonna pee

Que pass?
what's up ?
Example: Que pass? I'm doing great

seeyabye
good bye
Example: I'm going . seeyabye

smash hit
huge success
Example: If I can get that job , It will be a smash hit for me

suss out
find out , understand
Example: Is there anyone here who susses out English?

tube
television
Example: hey dude , turn on that damn tube

upchuck
to vomit, throw up
Example: frequently the sights I saw made me feel like upchucking

whats cooking?
what's up , how is everything
Example: what's cooking dude?

when hell freezes over
never
Example: hey do u wanna meet her tonight? when hell freezes over!

wiz
piss , urinate
Example: do you know a place here for making wiz?

yamop
means I'm just kidding.
Example: Paul you're the best looking guy in the world....yamop

yapper
Telephone, usually in reference to a cellular phone.
Example: Whose yapper's ringing?

yark
to talk and talk and talk without end.
Example: That woman over there is just yarking on and on about opera, it is
so annoying

yence
to screw something up really bad
Example: I totally yenced up the answer on the last essay question!

yeppers
yes
Example: yeppers, that's right.

yesbody
someone; antonym of nobody
Example: knock knock. A: Who's there? B: Yesbody.

yesh
Slang for yes.
Example: We gonna go see him today? yesh, indeed.

yonks
a long time
Example: Little Johnny waited for the train for yonks

You betcha!
yes (as in a strong positive response to a suggestion or an offer)
Example : will you drive ? you betcha!

yumhum
used when you are agreeing to something or saying yes
Example: are we going to the movies tonight? yumhum

yuppie gunfight
when two or more people reach for their cell phone when one rings. see also 'cellphonic appraisal'
Example: when Ron, Justin, and mike heard a cell phone ring, it was a yuppie gunfight to see who could grab their phone first.

yurp
to belch
Example: I say, don't yurp in front of my wife. Sorry, old chap, didn't realize it was her turn.

zippy
Okay or perfect
Example: It was a warm , sunny day , a zippy afternoon for a ballgame

zonk
to hit or punch someone
Example: she zonked him in the nose

People

Abal
Used by the younger generation to label a person as dumb, uncouth, unsophisticated.
Example: You're just an abal

able grable
a very pretty girl
Example: look at that able grable . she' s my
girlfriend

adorababe
Used when someone is both hot and cute.
Example: My girlfriend is perfect, she's adorababe.

ajax
An exceptionally attractive girl.
Example: Check out that girl, she's ajax.

anchovy
A young female age 13-25 who has no class. Girls
who act stupid and criticize others for doing the same.
Example: Check out that anchovy in the mini-skrit,
she's sitting with her legs open

ankle
nice girl
Example: my girl is a ankle

ark
nice girl
Example: have you ever seen that ark around here?

babe
a good-looking young woman
Example: he got married with a real babe

baby kisser
politician
Example : I hate baby kisser

bad news
wet blanket , one who spoils the other's happiness
Example: he 's such a bad news all the time

bagman
riffraff
Example: police arrested two bagman yesterday

ball of fire
active guy
Example: my dad is a ball of fire , that's why i like
him

bimbo
a pretty, but empty-headed, young lady
Example: we've got lots of bimbo in our university

blimp
fat guy
Example: you gotta lose some weight . your
becoming blimp man!

bloke
man
Example: whose that bloke over there?

bod
one guy
Example: the bod is coming is my friend . I know
him

careeput
stingy
Example: A: Buy me a drink? B: No. A: You're so
careeput

chaif
A beautiful girl that you would like to flirt with her
Example: lets go out and Chalk up some chaif's

chap
a man
Example: a chap in the blue car is my uncle

chatty kathy
A person who talks too much.
Example: The lady in the aisle seat was a chatty kathy

cheapskate
stingy guy
Example: Don't be a cheapskate and lend him some bucks

chick
girl
Example look at that chick over there

Chicka
A girl or woman that is especially beautiful and trendy.
Example: That girl is a fine chicka

chicklet, biblet
An annoying, bubbly, teenage girl.
Example: We've gotta jet--there's a pack of chicklets heading our way

Chickypoo
A pretty girl in unconventional attire.
Example: She may look weird, but she's a real chickypoo

chogret
A close friend.
Example: Hey, chogret, lets go to the mall tonight

chop
An absolute jerk. A person who thinks she is cool and has lots of friends. The truth is, nobody likes her.
Example: Pam is a chop. Why does she hang out with us when we tell her to go away?

chuddy
not really fat
Example: he 's got a chuddy baby

Coolio G-mony
man
Example: Well, all right, Coolio G-mony

crackerbarrel
An obese person or someone with a very large appetite; can be used as a noun, verb, or adjective.
Example: whenever he goes to party , he eats everything . he's a crackerbarrel

crackle
adjective used to describe a girl who is very beautiful
Example: Erin wasn't just pretty, she was crackle.

creep
unpleasant guy
Example: he 's kind a creep

cromulent
egotistical, arrogant, etc.
Example: That cromulent King, tells the people false information regarding taxes

crum-bum
Person who is dirty, lazy. Never leaves the house.
Example: Katie hasn't left her house in 4 days and she's kinda stinky. What a crum-bum!

crumbler
someone who hates everything and everybody
Example: when I was a kid , I was a crumbler and nobody could talk to me

cunny
a beautiful girl with attitude
Example: your new girl is a cunny and cool chick

Cuzzo
Cousin.
Example: What's up, cuzzo?

Daughter of Aphrodite
A female who is particularly beautiful; especially a young woman.
Example: Sarah Michelle Gellar is a daughter of Aphrodite

Defective Shake-N-Bake
One whose face 'peels' due to dryness or high acid acne medication.
Example: Look at Defective Shake-N-Bake over there

deniro jockey
A female who always expects the male to pay, whether he is her boyfriend or not.
Example: I'm broke, my deniro jockey has worn my wallet out

dept
Describing word for a guy, especially when he's looking his best.
Example: You're looking dept tonight, Jimmy , you shouldn't have any trouble meeting some new girls

dexterfreebish
snobbish
Example: Some rich kids are dexterfreebishes

dimbo
A mix of bimbo and dumb
Example: That blonde is such a dimbo. I can't believe she forgot the lid on the coffee cup again.

dimepiece
An attractive woman.
Example: Mary has a pretty face and curves in all the right places. She's definitely a dimepiece

Dinkum Thinkum
Sharp Thinker
Example: Mike was a fair Dinkum Thinkum, sharpest computer you'll ever meet

dole
Slang for unemployment.
Example: I'll never be able to work again , I've been so spoiled living on the dole

doof
Someone silly or funny.
Example: Chris thinks he's funny, but he's the wrong kind of doof

dorkana,dorkano
Used meaning stupid (in a funny way) or just not thinking
Example: Sally couldn't believe what a dorkano her friend was when he licked the ice cream store sign's large ice cream cone

dorkus ficus
A dork, nerd.
Example: Quit being such a dorkus ficus.

double digit
Not particularly intelligent, as in only two digits in her IQ
Example: She was so double digit, she couldn't finish middle school

drooly
A slang word for excessively cute
Example: there are lots of drooly out there . Let's go and tax their mind!

dude
man , friend
Example: hey , dude this party is boring

egli
Out of shape, fat, obese.
Example: Get off the couch. Exercise, jog, do some aerobics. For God's sake, do something. You're getting really egli.

Emotional Vampire
A person who sucks the energy right out of you.
Example: I was having a great day until all the emotional vampires at work arrived.

esbee-esspee
a close friend.
Example: I like Nicky--she's esbee-espee

fancy ones self
has a high opinion of herself
Example: she fancies hers self all the time

fashion chuck
a well dressed man
Example: When Matt walked into the bar he caught the eye of every lady. When he took off his jacket they could see right away he was a fashion chuck.

fatty
fat guy
Example: she 's so fatty and has got not any pal

feeb
One who is socially, mentally, and physically feeble.
Example: You didn't ask for her phone number? You're such a feeb

filth bucket
A really ugly girl
Example: Chris is usually attracted to filth buckets

fistaloar
Someone who likes to fight a lot.
Example: James got kicked out of school yesterday!
Yeah, he's a real fistaloar

flamed
the one who takes everything serious
Example: I was just kidding with you . don't be a
flamed

flat tire
dull
Example: Tom is a real flat tire

fluffy nazi
A girl who looks sweet and innocent but is really
Hitler in pumps.
Example: As I made Kevin fork over the red crayon
in kindergarden, I knew I would enjoy the power of
being a fluffy nazi.

flulu
person or place that appears to think highly of herself
or itself.
Example: In New York City, I frequently saw flulu
women dressed to the nines with their noses in the air.

gal
girl
Example: did you notice that gal in club yesterday?

hip-shooter
talk without thinking
Example: he's a hip-shooter

hog
who eats a lot
Example: my little sis is a hog

hoity toity
arrogant
Example: your friend introduced me to the other
guest who were all so hoity toity

honcho
boss
Example: who is the honcho here?

jock
an athlete, sportsman
Example: we have so many jock in our country

lardos
fat guy
Example: he is really lardos

leftie
pessimistic guy
Example: she's pretty leftie about her chances .

looker
a good-looking man or woman, an attractive person
Example: look at that looker out there .

loudmouth
an obnoxious person who talks too much and too
loudly
Example: stop being such a loudmouth .

namby-pamby
womanizer
Example: Jack is a namby-pamby person as I know

old man
father
Example: I love old men

ldie
old guy
Example: he's becoming oldie

quitter
a person who gives up easily when faced with a
difficult challenge
Example: he can't face with any difficulties . he's a
quitter person

skag
an ugly girl
Example: you wanna make friend with that skag girl?

steady
boyfriend and girlfriend
Example: finally , they got steady to each other

tail
a person who's following someone to find out where
they're going and what they're doing
Example: I hate who is tail all the time

uppity
conceited, arrogant, pretentious
Example: I never met a more uppity and arrogant young man .

wanker
an arrogant or pretentious person
Example: he's a great musician , and not wannker at all .

wannabe
one who wants to be rich or famous
Example: Jane is so wannabe . she has got a lots of huge dream in her mind

weirdo
very strange person
Example: don't talk to him . he seems like a weirdo

wimp
a weak, unassertive person
Example: that stupid boy is a wimp . he can't do anything wit his hands .

wrinklie
old guy
Example: my grand mom is a wrinklie

yahootie
A clumsy not so bright person.
Example: That yahootie spilled all the food on the floor

yardstick bubblegum
a very dirty male or female
Example: without that huge money , he looks like a
yardstick bubblegum

yob
looser , riffraff
Example: you can't find jack shit yob around our
new house

Risk

dicey
risky, unsafe, dangerous
Example: don't drive with this car . that's a dicey one

give one's eyetooth for something
to risk anything in order to obtain something
Example: I'd give my eyetooth to look like her

go for something
be courage about something
Example: It looks like a cop , just go for it

guts
courage
Example: I don't have guts to meet her anymore

hairy
dangerous
Example: we went on a trip with a hairy airplane

stick one's neck out for someone
to risk a lot
Example: I stuck my neck out for him

Sleep

aslake attack
When you are mostly asleep but partially awake and you suddenly twitch a body part because something in your almost dream did so.
Example: I had an aslake attack last night and involuntarily slapped myself in the head.

catch some Z's
get some sleep
Example: I need catch some Z's

cotched
to go to sleep
Example: I cotched on my floor the other night.

crack of noon
Sleeping in late
Example: I was up at the crack of noon.

crash out
go to sleep
Example: he crashed out when he was driving car

daymare
A nightmare that is lived out in the light of day; a bad dream come true.
Example: His daymare about her turned out to be far worse than any nightmare he could dream up.

don't sleep on
It means don't underestimate something or someone.
Example: Hey, don't sleep on Max . He's a strength
guy

flop out
to fall asleep almost instantly
Example: I was so tired the other day, I flopped out
as soon as I got home

grab forty winks
to take a nap
Example: I'm going to grab forty winks before we
leave

hit the sack
to go to bed
Example: hit the sack now . otherwise you will get
up late tomorrow

sack
a bed
Example: you've got a nice sack

shuteye
to go sleep
Example: I need get some shuteye

sleep in until noon
to sleep late until noon
Example: I got used to sleep in until noon last year

Zizz

to take a nap without going to bed.

Example: I was up all night so I zizzed at the monitor at work

Stomach

barf someone guts up

to vomit

Example: if you eat one more pizza , you will barf your guts up

basket

stomach

Example: I have a pain in my stomach

belly button

navel

Example: have you had a pain in your belly button

belly up

to fail

Example: the referee said you failed in this match .

bread basket

stomach

Example: oh my gosh , pain in my bread basket! .

bust a gut

to laugh hard

Example: he busted a gut laughing

floochie
a floochie is the act of placing one's mouth on someone else's stomach, arm, etc. and blowing out, for the purpose of making a phthhhh sound.
Example: Daddy's gonna give you a stomach floochie

get a gut
to get a big belly
Example: you are standing to get a gut

got the gut
courage
Example: could you talk to my daddy and tell him about my result's exam? I don't got the got .

gut
stomach
Example: the attacker kicked him in the stomach .

gutsy
to be courageous .
Example: she is very gutsy

hate someone's guts
to despise someone
Example hate her guts !

have guts to do something
have the courage to do something
Example: he has the guts to be a policeman .

pot belly
big stomach
Example: look at that guy over there with his pot belly .

spill ones guts
to disclose ones innermost feelings
Example: she spilled her guts to me

throw ones guts up
to vomit
Example: I threw my guts up after drinking those two beers .

unable to stomach someone or something
unable to tolerate someone or something
Example: I can 't stomach her .

Toilet

biffy
toilet
Example: where is the biffy

can
toilet, bathroom
Example: I should use the can before we leave

comfort station
toilet
Example: Do you have a comfort station in this store?

craphouse
toilet
Example: I'm looking for a craphouse

crapper
toilet
Example: where is the nearest crapper around here?

dunny
toilet
Example: could you tell me where is dunny around here?

gab room
women toilet
Example: She said , where is the nearest gab room around here

head
toilet
Example: I'm looking for a head

loo
toilet, bathroom
Example: I need loo now

Terl It
toilet
Example: I need to go to terl it